THE NEW DEAL
REVOLUTION OR EVOLUTION?

Problems in American Civilization

PREPARED UNDER THE EDITORSHIP OF

Earl Latham
George Rogers Taylor
George F. Whicher

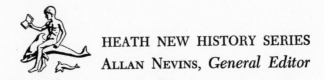

HEATH NEW HISTORY SERIES
ALLAN NEVINS, *General Editor*

The New Deal

REVOLUTION OR
EVOLUTION?

EDITED WITH AN INTRODUCTION BY

Edwin C. Rozwenc

Problems in American Civilization

READINGS SELECTED BY THE
DEPARTMENT OF AMERICAN STUDIES
AMHERST COLLEGE

D. C. HEATH AND COMPANY: Boston

Offices

| Boston | New York | Chicago | Dallas |
| Atlanta | San Francisco | London |

INTRODUCTION

A HISTORIAN finds it very difficult to think of any other administration in our history which affected the American people so powerfully and in so many different ways as the administrations of Franklin Delano Roosevelt. The Roosevelt New Deal was a period of unparalleled legislative activity, during which the laws enacted by the Congress were not only quantitatively more numerous than in any preceding period of our history, but also bewilderingly novel and complex. At the same time, the executive branch of the government underwent spectacular expansion, accompanied by an unprecedented multiplication of administrative rules and regulations.

In many ways the New Deal made far greater demands upon the citizen than any previous administration in our history. The voter who wished to keep intelligently informed of what his government was doing found it difficult to acquire an understanding of the Emergency Banking Act, the Glass-Steagall Act, the Gold Repeal Joint Resolution, the National Industrial Recovery Act, the Securities and Exchange Act, the Utilities Holding Company Act, the Agricultural Adjustment Act, the Soil Conservation and Domestic Allotment Act, the Farm Mortgage Refinancing Act, the Farm Mortgage Foreclosure Act, the National Labor Relations Act, the Fair Labor Standards Act, the Social Security Act, the Tennessee Valley Authority Act, the Reciprocal Trade Agreements Act — to name only some of the more outstanding pieces of legislation. Moreover, these laws tended to become lengthier and more involved until an act like the Agricultural Adjustment Act of 1938 filled 104 pages of relatively small print. Even a confirmed New Dealer could feel a little sympathy for the exasperated senator who assailed the Agricultural Adjustment Act of 1938 as the "most completely conglomerate mess of involved language which was ever perpetrated upon a free people!"

In addition, the conscientious citizen who wished to develop adequate political judgments experienced equal difficulty in making some sense out of the plethoric jumble of new administrative agencies, the names of which were abbreviated into such alphabetical designations as AAA, WPA, PWA, CWA, REA, TVA, SEC, NLRB, FSA, UHA, FHA, CAA, CCC, RA, FDIC, NRA, NYA, HOLC. The dominant letter in most of these kaleidoscopic alphabetical combinations was A — for ADMINISTRATION — although there were those who preferred to spell it with a B — for BUREAUCRACY. In any case, it appeared that administration or bureaucracy was here to stay as one result of the New Deal.

Of course, to understand fully the intent of the New Deal laws and the objectives of the New Deal administrators, the conscientious citizen needed to acquaint himself with the economic and sociological meanings of such terms as "parity payments," "industrial unionism," "codes of fair competition," "processing tax," "migratory agricultural labor," "share-croppers," "subsistence homestead," "mortgage refinancing," "death sentence clause," "ever-normal granary," "marketing orders." These strenuous obligations of citizenship had a lighter side, too, with the rich flowering of a new political vocabulary which included such memorable words and phrases as "chiseling," "social neanderthal," "boondoggling," "economic royalists," "horse and buggy days," "baloney dollar," and "recession." On the whole, informed citizenship was beginning to require something approaching the training of a college major in the social sciences.

Even if the average American made no effort to keep up fully with the legislative and administrative activities of the national government, he became more and more aware personally of the expanding power of the government. No longer did his formal relationship to the government consist of purchasing a postage stamp or filling out an income tax return. The federal government was invading the daily lives and activities of businessmen, farmers, and laborers through collective bargaining guarantees, deduction of social security taxes from payrolls, marketing orders, relief payments, benefit payments, home loans, bank deposit guarantees, the fixing of minimum wages and maximum hours, and the extraction of truth about securities. And, if not everyone agreed that this was a brave new world, there was no one who could deny that it was certainly different from American life in the earlier periods of our history.

All of this tremendous legislative activity and administrative energy went on in an atmosphere of acute social tension. The New Deal was a response — almost frantic at times — to a terrible economic crisis which not only had checked seriously the remarkable economic expansion which had characterized the historical growth of America, but also had destroyed the superior standard of living of a large segment of our population and with it the three-centuries-old vision of America as the promised land. The New Deal, by its vigorous attacks upon a large number of domestic problems, made available many social benefits to distressed classes of people, and, for many, restored faith in American democracy. Yet it would be foolhardy to say that the buoyant optimism which had characterized the American mind before 1929 was restored. The fighting faith in America which Americans took up again in the thirties was tempered by the realization that we had been precariously close to economic disaster in 1933 and that we could never consider ourselves out of danger as long as ten million or more Americans were unemployed. In many ways, the New Deal marks the beginning for Americans of the deep social anxiety which the ensuing world crisis seems to have fixed as the permanent fate of man in the twentieth century.

Now, for the first time, it is possible for Americans to begin to evaluate the New Deal in the perspective of the whole historical development of the United States. The experience of World War II and its aftermath enables us to fix more clearly the chronological bounds of the New Deal era. As a definable political period it belongs to the 1930's and, even though much of the New Deal program and philosophy has continued, our immediate decade appears to be a separate political era which has to be defined in terms of the world situation.

When one begins to examine the New Deal in perspective, the question inevitably arises — what did this tremendous outpouring of legislation, this ubiquitous infiltration of American life by an army of administrators armed to the teeth with clerical forms, mean in relation to the full sweep of our historical experience? Was the New Deal the beginning of a completely new tack in the course of American development or was it merely a twentieth century elaboration of democratic and reformist ideas which can be traced back through the American tradition to the American Revolution? Was the New Deal, in other words, an evolutionary culmination of a long historical process, or was it the beginning of a new departure — "a peaceable revolution"?

Of course, at this point, one is reminded of the bitter political controversy which accompanied the New Deal. As a matter of fact, one of the distinguishing characteristics of the New Deal era was the high level of political tension with practically no real lulls in political conflict after 1934. During those years of heated controversy it became commonplace for the political opposition to charge the Roosevelt administration with revolutionary intent and to characterize the President as a "dictator." The succeeding years have witnessed gradually cooling passions, but a sharp division of outlook continues.

Even with the insulation of an elapsed decade between us and the New Deal period, a well-known American historian, writing dispassionately of the New Deal in relation to the "shaping of the American tradition," has come to the conclusion that the New Deal was a peaceable revolution. The selection from Louis M. Hacker's *The Shaping of the American Tradition* which stands first in the readings below develops the main arguments in support of the thesis that the New Deal constitutes a "third American Revolution."

Professor Hacker's historical judgment is at sharp variance with that of his colleague at Columbia University, Henry Steele Commager. The latter maintains that the New Deal was simply a notably successful and creative period in the evolution of the American reformist tradition. Professor Commager's article, "Twelve Years of Roosevelt," included in the selections, develops the evidence for this emphasis on continuity in the historical interpretation of the New Deal.

On the whole, it would be fair to say that Professor Commager's opinion was shared by the majority of the supporters of the New Deal. In the earlier political battles of the thirties, the advocates of the New Deal found this kind of appeal to the American reformist tradition to be a useful counter to the traditionalism of the Republican opposition. Yet one of the more interesting criticisms of the attempt to link the New Deal with our reformist tradition was made by a noted political commentator who had played a part in the development of that tradition. Walter Lippmann, writing "The Permanent New Deal" in 1935, admitted that it would be an "exaggeration" to say that the regulatory measures, the conservation program, or even the social insurance program represented a clean break with the past; but he maintained that certain other aspects of the New Deal were "new" and "radical." Mr. Lippmann's analysis of these radical innovations is the third selection in this volume.

To give the creator of the New Deal a chance to speak for himself, three public addresses by Franklin D. Roosevelt have been included in the readings, two from the election campaigns of 1932 and 1936 and the third delivered during the bitter fight over the reorganization of the judiciary. The selection has been guided by the purpose of revealing what Roosevelt thought about the relationship between social and political innovation and our basic democratic traditions.

The New Deal ran into a considerable amount of crossfire from both the right and the left during the exciting days of the thirties. In our readings the views of conservatives are reflected in a selection from Herbert Hoover's book, *The Challenge to Liberty*, written during Roosevelt's first administration. An excerpt from a speech by Earl Browder after Roosevelt's re-election in 1936 expresses the attitude of American communists.

The readings close with selections from the work of three historians who have recently been making close studies of Roosevelt and the New Deal. The analyses by Basil Rauch, Arthur M. Schlesinger, Jr., and Richard Hofstadter furnish some valuable insights into Roosevelt's program.

In one sense, the problem posed by this volume can be reduced to the old pedagogical question of whether to stress differences or similarities in comparing historical periods. No doubt a skeptic would smile with detached amusement at this game which historians like to play. Nevertheless, the attempt to discover whether the relationship of the New Deal period to the rest of our history is primarily a revolutionary or an evolutionary one can help us to understand where we are today and where we may be going.

[NOTE: The anecdote by Frances Perkins on p. x is quoted from *The Roosevelt I Knew* (New York, 1946), p. 330, by permission of the Viking Press.]

CONTENTS

The Clash of Issues

In 1934 Herbert Hoover said:

> National Regimentation [under the New Deal] . . . is a vast shift from the American concept of human rights which even the government may not infringe to those social philosophies where men are wholly subjective to the state. It is a vast casualty to Liberty if it shall be continued.

Looking back a dozen years later, Louis M. Hacker concluded:

> A revolution was started by the New Deal — not a revolution in the violent, turbulent sense, but a revolution nevertheless.

On the other hand, Henry Steele Commager insists:

> We can see now [1945] that the "Roosevelt Revolution" was no revolution, but rather the culmination of half a century of historical development.

What Franklin D. Roosevelt thought about his program is suggested by the following story told by Frances Perkins:

> A superficial young reporter once said to Roosevelt . . . , "Mr. President, are you a Communist?"
> "No."
> "Are you a capitalist?"
> "No."
> "Are you a Socialist?"
> "No," he said, with a look of surprise as if he were wondering what he was being cross-examined about.
> The young man said, "Well, what is your philosophy then?"
> "Philosophy?" asked the President, puzzled. "Philosophy? I am a Christian and a Democrat — that's all."

Louis M. Hacker:

THE THIRD AMERICAN REVOLUTION

The Election of Franklin
  Delano Roosevelt

For Americans who took pride in the possession of their own homes and automobiles, who sent their children to high schools and colleges, who moved in a complex and satisfying social round of fraternal meetings, church suppers, and outdoor games, to see — as was happening so widely during 1930–33 — their security shaken, their possessions and small savings melting away, their lives becoming more secret and lonely, their children leaving home before educations had been completed — these were profound traumatic experiences. The great majority of Americans were the humble, the hardworking, the thrifty — the workers, the small farmers, the little retailers, professional and technical men, the smaller manufacturers. It is small wonder that they flocked to the support of the new President and his policies. Franklin D. Roosevelt and the New Deal restored the confidence of the typical American in himself and in his country's destiny. This was achievement, even if many of the programs failed or fell short of their purpose and even if the end-results seemed to threaten unknown perils. Americans had at least learned that their political institutions and Constitutional processes could bend without breaking, and that

what a people needed was courage — and that they had.

THE CAMPAIGN OF 1932. The depression was in its third year when the presidential contest of 1932 took place. The Republicans renamed President Hoover and Vice President Curtis as their standard bearers. The Democrats nominated Governor Franklin D. Roosevelt of New York for the presidency and Speaker John N. Garner of Texas for the vice presidency. Roosevelt's campaign captured the country's imagination. Beginning in the spring of 1932, he traveled more than 25,000 miles and visited almost every state in the Union; and he talked openly and freely of fundamental economic problems. One clearcut distinction between the positions of the two candidates quickly began to emerge. Hoover attributed the depression to international factors; Roosevelt tended to stress the difficulties and faults in our own economy. It was hard to assume — and none but the most partisan did so — that Roosevelt was hostile to the American capitalist system. But he did look forward to a capitalist system severely modified and limited, hedged around closely in the interests of the security of the workingman, farmer, small homeowner, and small investor. And its activities were to be directed so completely to the attainment of social rather than individual ends that to many who had been brought up on the concepts of a laissez-faire society and an automatically self-adjusting economy a real revolution threatened.

THE THIRD AMERICAN REVOLUTION. These, as it turned out, were not false prophets. A revolution was started by the New Deal — not a revolution in the violent, turbulent sense, but a revolution nevertheless. The whole concept of the state, or national government, underwent a metamorphosis. The state had previously been a passive or impartial force, seeking to stand aloof from the contests in the market place, or at best offering only its mediation to see that principles of justice and equity were preserved; and it had refused to interfere significantly in the interests of the security and the welfare of its laboring peoples. Now it became the interventionist state. It imposed on the free business enterpriser all sorts of controls and regulations; it entered openly into business itself, often as competitor with private corporations; it used its great fiscal and financial powers to redistribute wealth and to create income; it committed itself to an elaborate program of social security that offered protection, in time, to the whole population against the mischances of unemployment, invalidity, and sudden death, and from the cradle to the grave. The laissez-faire state with only a skeletal apparatus of offices and agencies had become the social-service state with a vast and intricately contrived and permanent machinery of officials and bureaucrats.

And political power, too, had shifted. Previously political power had been in the hands of the middle class — the industrialists, the bankers, the larger farmers. Now political power was concentrating more and more in the hands of the lower middle class and the workers.

Those who voted for Franklin D. Roosevelt in 1932, 1936, 1940, and 1944 came from the smaller farmers throughout the country; from the urban dwellers who toiled as workers and salaried employees; from small distributors, small manufacturers, and those on the WPA rolls. Interestingly enough, this took place without a break-up and redistribution in national party formations and without the appearance of a workingmen's political party.

FROM A NATIONALIST TO AN INTERNATIONALIST ORIENTATION. Furthermore, the revolution took place despite the fact that the pivot of its operations changed. The New Deal started out by being essentially nationalist in its outlook and interests, and continued so until 1937. From 1937 on, it became increasingly internationalist. And yet the fundamental political and social philosophy remained the same. The American state was to be used for security and welfare; this could be done by re-ordering our domestic economy without any real concern over what was happening outside our shores — so ran the thinking and planning of the New Deal up to 1937. The American state was to be used for security and welfare; but we could not be free to handle the problems of high employment and of improving standards of living until the whole world was made safe from aggression; and freedom from want and fear could not be assured Americans unless all peoples were similarly guaranteed these rights — thus ran the philosophy of the New Deal from 1937 on. The same groups, by and large, who had supported the New Deal in its first stage followed its leadership in the second.

As the presidential campaign of 1932 drew out its term, it became apparent that Roosevelt was to be elected by an overwhelming majority. And so it turned out. He received 22,800,000 popular votes to Hoover's 15,800,000, and 472 electoral votes to Hoover's 59. The Republican ticket carried only the six states of Maine, New Hampshire, Vermont, Connecticut, Pennsylvania, and Delaware. The Democrats also elected heavy majorities to both houses of Congress.

Theory and Tactics of the New Deal

THEORY OF THE NEW DEAL. Some of the New Deal policies were understood and acted upon at once; some were adopted only to be abandoned later; some were originally primary and then were pushed into the background. Some were improvisations devised on the spot; and some went as far back as Populism and the New Freedom for their inspiration. Always, however, there existed the thought that the responsibility of public authority for the welfare of the people was clear and that the intervention of the state was justifiable. The theoretical bases of New Deal policy may be put down in this fashion:

1. Capital plant at home had presumably over-expanded as far as the normal requirements for agricultural and industrial goods were concerned; investment therefore was no longer to be the exclusive concern of private banking. This theory was pushed most energetically in the field of agriculture, where limitation of production became the basis of policy. That it also was extended to industry was evident from the codes of "fair competition" written during 1933–35 under the National Industrial Recovery Act. Under these, many industries, in the process of policing themselves, were permitted to provide for rigorous controls over the use of existing machinery and over new-plant expansion. The idea also colored trade-union policy, for unions were allowed to impose limitations upon production through so-called feather-bed jobs, full-crew requirements, and similar devices. From this con-

ception of overexpansion there followed the New Deal theory of social investment as complementary and sometimes in opposition to private investment.

2. Prices were being "managed," or they were "sticky" in significant areas of business operations. The New Deal held that this was due to monopolistic practices and to imperfect competition, that is to say, to conscious interference with the free movement of prices on the part of corporations. A bold attack on monopoly practices was therefore in order.

3. Labor had an inadequate share of the national income on the one hand, and unequal bargaining powers in industrial relations on the other. Both conditions could be remedied by compelling the legal recognition of trade unions and by legislation fixing minimum wages and maximum hours of work.

4. Business enterprises in many fields had become "overcapitalized," in the sense that their fixed charges due to capital costs were higher than would permit the concerns affected to operate profitably. Since such costs did not adjust easily and quickly to changed market conditions, the difficulties of total market adjustment were intensified. Debt revisions were therefore in order.

5. The public-utilities industry, furnishing electric power and light, which was notably under corporate control, was not favorably disposed to a vast expansion program to reach potential users and isolated communities. At this point was introduced a bold piece of social engineering — the Tennessee Valley Authority.

6. The toll taken by unemployment, cyclical as well as technological (although on the latter point there was much debate), was very great. There were other insecurities which philanthropy and private savings were inadequate to cope with: old age, invalidity, child dependency, sudden death. Security to the American population against these perils was a prime concern of government.

7. There were dark spots in our economy: inadequate housing for low-income earners,

the plight of sharecroppers and agricultural laborers, unemployed youth. Here too was a field for state intervention.

8. The financial mechanism of banking and credit was too powerful an agency to be left entirely in private hands. Banking had to be made at least a semipublic function, so that banking policy could lead positively in controlling the ups and downs of business fluctuations.

9. The world market was no longer functioning properly; high tariff walls, import quota systems, foreign governmental controls, and the manipulations of foreign exchange prevented the usual absorption of American surpluses in foreign trade. Our cotton, cereals, tobacco, oil, copper were piling up in warehouses to derange markets at home. Two lines of attack were indicated: controlled production, and the elimination of those blocks that were hindering the orderly processes of world trade.

TACTICS OF THE NEW DEAL. So ran the New Deal analysis. From this there followed certain programs, of which the following were the outstanding:

1. The restoration and maintenance of prices. Many attacks on the problem were launched: the dollar was devaluated; gold was purchased from abroad; limitations were imposed on the production of agricultural products, petroleum, and coal; codes of fair competition in industry were written to eliminate cutthroat methods. The greatest success was met with in the case of agriculture, although here crop loans and subsidies were also required for the purpose of making production control effective.

2. The reduction of debt. Private debts had become unduly burdensome, notably within the context of a deflationary price situation. The New Deal sought to come to grips with this problem in two ways: by raising prices, and by writing down the face value of debt in places where price change itself could not be entirely and immediately effective. For agriculture it created a new

fiscal agency (the Federal Farm Mortgage Corporation) which was to make possible the exchange of privately held agricultural long-term paper for semipublic (or public-guaranteed) paper. For homeowners it created a new fiscal agency (the Home Owners' Loan Corporation) for a similar purpose. For businessmen, corporations, and municipalities, it radically changed the bankruptcy law to permit those who were insolvent to come to an understanding with their creditors quickly and at small legal cost.

3. The revival and expansion of credit. To pump short-term and long-term funds into enterprise, state intervention was imperative. The commercial banks, because of their nonliquidity, were not in a position to extend loans for working capital. The agencies of long-term credit — savings banks, insurance companies, trust companies, title and mortgage companies — seeing their earlier investments unproductive, feared to assume further risks. The New Deal jumped into the breach. It expanded the powers and operations of the Reconstruction Finance Corporation (created in 1932 to open commercial banks and help them achieve liquidity quickly). It established virtual public control over the Federal Reserve System, so that the system could be induced by government policy to expand (and contract) credit. It obtained for the Board of Governors of the Federal Reserve System the power to lower (and raise) the minimum legal reserves required of member banks. It got for the same agency the right to raise (or lower) the margin requirements for security purchases, thus controlling to an extent the amount of credit flowing into brokers' loans. It used the Reconstruction Finance Corporation to make direct loans to private business and to municipalities and other public corporations for housing, electric power plants, and the like.

4. The raising of the purchasing power of labor. Labor, confronted by shrinking opportunities of employment, was forced to sell its services cheaply. Sweated industries

had reappeared and child labor had increased. The key to the rehabilitation of labor was to be chiefly its own united strength. The National Labor Relations Act therefore ordered employers to bargain with the workers' own trade unions and to give up practices that prevented labor organization. Closed shops became more and more common; and also industrial practices and standards were modified and improved through labor-management cooperation. To defend those incapable of effective organization — children, women, the unskilled — minimum-wage and maximum-hour legislation and the abolition of child labor were aimed at. After several failures these objectives were achieved in the Fair Labor Standards Act of 1938.

5. The relief of the needy, the protection of dependents, and social security. Wholesale unemployment, illness and invalidity, and the unrest of youth were the results of the depression. The relief of distress was an imminent public duty, and the New Deal experimented with this problem in many ways. It lent generously to the states for straight outdoor relief. It created a federal agency (the Public Works Administration) to extend credit to public and quasi-public authorities to finance long-term public construction projects. It wrote Social Security legislation under which direct federal appropriations and federal matching grants-in-aid were made to the states to provide for the unemployables and the permanently needy (the aged, the blind, dependent and crippled children). It devised a significant code under which, as a result of contributions by employers, unemployment funds were built up in the states; and also, from equal contributions by employers and workers, an insurance fund from which were to be paid annuities to workers upon retirement. It created work for the temporary needy and unemployed in short-term projects financed by the Federal government (under the Works Progress Administration).

6. The construction of homes. The New Deal recognized that the building of decent homes for low-income earners was an outstanding social need; it therefore established an agency (the United States Housing Authority) which, with government financing and subsidies, was to assist quasi-public authorities to create low-cost housing.

7. The protection of the investor and the saver. To defend the property rights of the American investor the New Deal set up the Securities and Exchange Commission and gave it wide powers to supervise the issuance of new securities by corporations, to obtain for investors adequate information about the financial practices of corporations and their directors and officers, and to regulate the functioning of brokers and the security exchanges, or markets, themselves. Similarly, the Federal Deposit Insurance Corporation was devised to guarantee deposits in savings banks accounts up to $5,000.

8. The rehabilitation of the electric power industry. Believing that an outlet for savings and a work of social reconstruction could be achieved in an expanded electric light and power industry, the New Deal created the Tennessee Valley Authority. The stated purposes were the rehabilitation of the population of the Tennessee Valley and the establishment of an experiment in the public operation of electric light and power. Focusing its attention on this industry as an example of banking domination, the New Deal also provided for the elimination of unnecessary holding companies.

9. The revival of foreign trade. The decline of foreign trade was a characteristic of our unbalanced economy. The New Deal sought to revive American overseas commerce; and for this purpose it created the Export-Import Bank to finance the flow of goods and even to extend credits to foreign governments. But the New Deal was equally interested in the restoration of world trade generally. Congress was therefore prevailed upon to permit the writing of reciprocal trading agreements with foreign nations as an executive function. Through the agency of the State Department (and without Senate

participation) a large number of such commercial treaties was drawn up, the net effect of which was the measurable lowering of tariff barriers. These agreements also contained most-favored-nation clauses.

10. Pump priming. When private enterprise failed to respond immediately or when business activity became sluggish, the New Deal proceeded to lend and spend. This it called "priming the pump"; in other words, the Federal government boldly engaged in deficit financing in an effort to raise national income. It lent to distressed banks, railroads, insurance companies, mortgage corporations, and industrial concerns; and to farmers, homeowners, the states, municipalities, and newly created public authorities. It spent — by subsidies, grants-in-aid, outright appropriations — in order to rehabilitate marginal farmers, to finance the building of ships, to tear down slums and put up low-rent housing, to furnish old-age pensions, to construct public buildings, and to provide flood control, roads, and reforestation. It not only gave people work, but at the same time added to the social wealth of the nation. This meant a steady increase in the national debt, a situation which the New Deal faced with equanimity because its theory of deficit financing was based on the premises that governmental spending made for an increase in national income and that an increase in national income made greater taxation possible. The nation was going into debt, it was true; but the debt was largely held at home, and, as a result of the debt, the country's assets had been increased. (So argued, at any rate, these new economics doctors.)

The New Deal Agencies

Such were the general New Deal policies and tactics designed to restore the American economy and make possible its smooth functioning, this time with more equity as far as the great masses of the country's population were concerned. A fuller description of some of the legislative enactments and the agencies set up is now in order.

AGRICULTURE. Because its condition was critical, agriculture received the immediate, and the continuing, attention of the New Deal. The goals for recovery and reform were the following: (1) The establishment of parity prices, that is, the restoration of the farmer's purchasing power to the position it had held in the immediate prewar years. The period of August, 1909, to July, 1914, was fixed on as the base period, the assumption being that at that time the prices farmers paid were in balance with the prices they received. (2) The establishment of parity income. This concept later on replaced the concept of parity prices. It was the intention of the Department of Agriculture to obtain for agriculture the relative income, as compared with total national income, which it had been receiving in the prewar years. (3) The adjustment of farm production to meet market requirements. This meant chiefly adjustment to domestic consumption. Production was therefore curtailed and where surpluses appeared, they were to be held off the market by means of government loans. Justification for this attitude was subsequently found in the concept of the "ever-normal granary." (4) Soil conservation and improvement of land use. (5) Debt reduction and security against foreclosure at the hands of mortgagees. (6) Rural relief and rehabilitation for submarginal farmers and tenants.

The first legislative enactment to carry out the major intention of this program was the Agricultural Adjustment Act, which was passed in May, 1933, and continued on the statute books until January, 1936. It must be repeated that the underlying conception was that agricultural distress was due to overproduction, not to underconsumption; therefore the growers of the basic staples were to be induced to restrict plantings, ultimately on the basis of a quota system. As compensation they were to receive subsidies ("benefit payments") and crop loans, the government holding the surpluses off the market. This was for the purpose of raising the prices of agricultural goods; and they were raised. The original AAA tied together the subsidies with a processing tax on millers, meat packers, cotton ginners, and so on, and, principally for this reason, was found unconstitutional by the Supreme Court.

To get around the objections of the Court there were passed the temporary Soil Conservation and Domestic Allotment Act of 1936 and the Agricultural Adjustment Act of 1938. In both these measures the justification for governmental action was found in the necessity for protecting the land resources of the nation and for encouraging the utilization of improved methods of cultivation. Again subsidies — this time directly — and crop loans were to be the basic instruments for obtaining compliance. The purpose of the commodity loans was to lay a floor below which farm prices could not fall.

Other major agricultural programs have already been noticed. The Emergency Farm Mortgage Act of 1933 was followed by the Farm Mortgage Refinancing Act of 1934, which created the Federal Farm Mortgage Corporation, under the direction of the Farm Credit Administration. The FFMC was given a revolving fund of two billion dollars in bonds, guaranteed as to principal and interest, which it could exchange for the bonds held by federal land banks and which it also could invest directly in farm mortgage loans. The FFMC succeeded in obtaining interest reductions and in scaling down the principal of farm obligations. After a series of unsuccessful experiments with resettlement projects,

the Farm Security Administration was finally set up in 1937 to devise ways and means of bringing relief to distressed small farmers and agricultural laborers; the chief method employed was rehabilitation through social-service activities. This, too, worked out well.

INDUSTRY. The revival of industry was to be pushed chiefly through price-raising expedients; but industry was to police itself, in order to eliminate unfair methods of competition. Despite the fact that a major commitment of American industrial policy was the Sherman Anti-Trust Act, the New Deal was prepared to welcome the cartelization of American business. For this purpose, the National Industrial Recovery Act was passed in June, 1933. It set up a National Recovery Administration, under whose aegis every branch of American business was to form code authorities, and these code authorities were to draw up principles and practices guaranteeing "fair competition." Most of these codes, when completed, incorporated methods for establishing minimum prices and restricting production. In May, 1935, the Supreme Court — incidentally, to everyone's relief — found the NIRA unconstitutional on three grounds: that Congress could not delegate its legislative powers to private individuals, that is, the code authorities; that the Federal government could not legislate about industrial practices if these practices did not directly affect interstate commerce; and that a national emergency did not exist. The administration then returned to a vigorous enforcement of the antitrust laws.

LABOR. The NIRA had incorporated and had made possible the establishment of certain fundamental rights of labor. Section 7(a) of the law had given workers the right to establish collective-bargaining agencies of their own choosing and had promised them minimum rates of pay, maximum hours of work, and other safeguards. The forty-hour week was generally established; minimum wages in most industries were put at between $12 and $15 a week; and the labor of children under sixteen years was banned.

The outlawing of the NIRA by the Supreme Court compelled the writing of new labor enactments. These took the form of the National Labor Relations Act in 1935 and the Fair Labor Standards Act (Wages and Hours Act) in 1938. The first was a great triumph for the country's workers and, indeed, was one of the outstanding achievements of the New Deal. It was frankly labor-oriented in that it was concerned only with industry's duties toward the workers: employers were obliged to bargain collectively with their employees and to give up all those industrial practices which might prevent the employees from properly realizing the objective of free trade-unionism. A specified number of unfair practices on the part of employers was accordingly rendered illegal. Also, when the workers were ready, they could call for an election to determine which trade union was to represent them in their negotiations with the employers. And finally, the National Labor Relations Board was set up, with wide powers. The board could decide which was to be the appropriate unit for the purposes of collective bargaining, that is, whether the unit was to be an employer unit, a craft unit, a plant unit, or even a regional unit. The board was to conduct elections. It was to certify the trade unions duly chosen by the majority of workers involved as exclusive bargaining agencies. And it was to prevent unfair labor practices by the use of quasi-judicial powers

similar to those exercised by the Federal Trade Commission in its own field.

The NLRB quickly received the cooperation of most employers. In a group of notable decisions in 1937, the Supreme Court validated the law. Indeed, the Court stretched the Constitutional concept of "interstate commerce" to such a degree that the NLRB's intervention in all labor disputes was made possible. Labor itself rose to its opportunity, and whereas in 1929 there were only 4,330,000 trade unionists in the country, at the end of the 1930s their numbers exceeded 11,000,000. Improvements in wage rates followed; and so did improvements in industrial relations, the outstanding new development being labor-management cooperation.

The Fair Labor Standards Act of 1938 was one of the country's most important pieces of welfare legislation. It established the forty-hour week, with time and a half for overtime, for all the country's industries. It provided for the creation of boards in all trades and businesses, which from time to time were to draw up minimum wage scales in order to "reach . . . the objective of a universal minimum wage of 40 cents an hour for each industry." And it virtually made possible the abolition of child labor by departmental order (in this case, the order of the Department of Labor).

SOCIAL SECURITY. The Social Security Act of 1935 (amended in 1939) permitted the United States to catch up with those European countries that had pioneered in the field of social security some twenty-five years earlier. The act made provisions for the following: (1) An Old-Age and Survivors' insurance program, administered by the Federal government. Many categories of workers, in establishments employing eight or more persons, were to be assured retirement allowances at sixty-five years of age and after. The fund was to be built up by matching contributions from the workers and employers; and this contribution was initially put at 1 percent, for each, of wages and earnings up to $3,000 a year. Benefit payments were to be based on marital status, length of coverage, and the size of the over-all contributions. Dependent survivors were also to be provided for. (2) A program of unemployment compensation, to be administered in every case by the states themselves. Through the agency of a federal payroll tax of 3 percent on payrolls, as a compulsory device, states were to be encouraged to set up unemployment-insurance schemes. It is enough to say that all did so; that in most cases the contributions to the maintenance of these funds were coming from the employers alone; and that benefit payments ran from fourteen to sixteen weeks, with an initial maximum weekly benefit of about $15 and a minimum weekly benefit of $5. (3) Federal grants to states, more or less on a matching basis, to take care of outstanding problems of dependency. These included assistance to the needy aged, the needy blind, and to children under sixteen deprived of parental support; and also grants for the establishment of maternal and child-health services, medical and other services for crippled children, and welfare services for the care of homeless, dependent, and neglected children. A Social Security Board was provided to administer most of the provisions of the law. In May, 1937, in three important decisions, the Supreme Court gave its stamp of approval to the Act.

CURRENCY AND CREDIT. Currency expansion and bank-credit inflation were major preoccupations of the New Deal.

In April, 1933, the United States formally went off the gold standard when an executive order stopped the free movement of gold both within and without the country. Congress gave its authorization through the passage of the Gold Repeal Joint Resolution of June, 1933, which canceled the gold clause in all federal and private obligations. A step in the direction of increasing the amount of money in circulation was taken with the passage of the Thomas Amendment to the AAA in May, 1933. This permitted the President to issue up to $3,000,000,000 worth of United States notes; to reduce the gold content of the dollar as much as 50 percent; and to accept silver from foreign governments on the account of the intergovernmental debts, as well as to buy American-mined silver. In January, 1934, Congress enacted the Gold Reserve Act, and under it the President fixed the value of the dollar at 59.06 cents in terms of its old parity; in other words, the government was permitted to buy gold anywhere at $35 an ounce. The hopes here were two: to push prices up by devaluation and to give the United States an advantage in foreign trade.

Bank-credit expansion was linked with banking reform. The Banking Act of 1933 and the Banking Act of 1935 provided for the following changes in the country's banking policy: (1) A Federal Deposit Insurance Corporation, already referred to, was set up. (2) Banks belonging to the Federal Reserve System were to cut themselves off from their securities affiliates. (3) The government's hold on the Federal Reserve System was greatly extended through the creation of the Board of Governors of the System, all of whom were to be appointed by the President. (4) The Open-Market Committee was to be dominated by the Board of Governors and was to have control over the powers of expanding and contracting credit. (5) The Board of Governors was also given the right to raise (or lower) reserve requirements of member banks and to raise (or lower) margin requirements on security purchases. Credit expansion was pushed also through government loans, notably by the use of the RFC.

POWER AND HOUSING. The Tennessee Valley Authority was established in May, 1933; its powers have been alluded to above. In the domain of power control, extensive reforms were launched. The Public Utility Act of 1935 had two functions: to expand the authority of the Federal Power Commission over all utilities transmitting electricity across state lines; and to give the SEC the right to put an end to holding companies in the utility field.

Many acts were passed in the field of housing. The Home Owners' Loan Act of April, 1934, came to the relief of existing and would-be small homeowners, by permitting the refinancing of outstanding mortgage debt and by creating facilities for the financing of new home construction. The National Housing Act of June, 1934, set up the Federal Housing Administration to standardize methods of construction and financing for multiple dwellings. The United States Housing Authority (under an act of 1937, amended in 1938) was to make loans to local public bodies, created by state law, to provide low-rent housing and slum clearance.

PUBLIC WORKS AND RELIEF. The New Deal sought to stimulate recovery by embarking on elaborate public-works projects. For this it received authority in the National Industrial Recovery Act, and the Public Works Administration was accordingly set up and given $3,000,000,000. But the programs moved tardily, with the result that in 1935 the

administration began to put its reliance increasingly on the less expensive "madework" projects of the Works Progress Administration. It was a considerable length of time before a proper program was devised to handle the case of the temporarily unemployed. In May, 1933, the Federal Emergency Relief Administration was set up; in October, 1933, there appeared the Civil Works Administration; and finally, in July, 1935, the Works Progress Administration. The WPA functioned well, not only making possible considerable additions to public plants but also providing employment as a substitute for outdoor relief. As for the unemployables, they were being handled by local home-relief agencies.

FINANCING THE NEW DEAL. The New Deal sought to charm back recovery by lending and spending on a vast scale. Up to 1935, the government made no serious effort to finance its spending program through taxation; and though after 1935 there was a good deal of tinkering with revenue acts, no new tax avenues were really explored. Deficit financing meant chiefly federal borrowings; as a result, the national debt steadily mounted.

The Progress of Recovery

THE COURSE OF BUSINESS. The New Deal's spending and easy-money programs and its own confidence in the essential soundness of America's institutions slowly spread the processes of revival. Agriculture was the first to respond, but the country's industry was not slow to follow; so that up to the midsummer of 1937 (except for a brief recession in 1934) the course of business activity moved upward. By 1937, the general level of production reached the average normal of the 1920s. This is not to assume that recovery was complete, for it was not. In fact, recovery was slower in the United States than in any other industrial country. Thus industrial production was almost as high as it had been in 1929; but on the basis of past performances it should have been higher, for the population of the country was greater and the rate of productivity in industry was perhaps 25 percent higher.

The upshot was that the spring of 1937, according to the American Federation of Labor's estimates, still saw 9,700,000 persons out of work. Why was this? A number of reasons may be adduced. (1) The government's spending and lending policy frightened off new business investment. To this degree the popular charge that there was a strike of capital was true. (2) Whereas labor had before been receiving an inadequate share of the national income, under the New Deal its share probably was too great. This increased the costs of production. (3) There was no real revival in our foreign trade, largely because of the national-economic policies pursued by most of the countries of Europe.

In agriculture, thanks to the subsidy, loan, and controlled-production measures of the New Deal, definite improvement had occurred. In 1932 the cash income from the sale of farm products had been $4,300,000,000; in 1937, the income from sales and government payments was $8,500,000,000 (government payments, or subsidies, were in the neighborhood of $500,000,000 yearly). The ratio of prices received to prices paid – the index of agricultural well-being – had moved up hearteningly. In 1932 the ratio stood at 61; that is, the farmer's dollar, in terms of the goods and services he could get for it, was worth 61 cents. In 1937, the ratio stood at 93. Farm real-estate values also mounted.

THE NATIONAL INCOME. Also, by 1937 and again by 1939, the country had recovered much of the position lost as a result of the depression in terms of its national income. From the low of 40 billions of dollars reached in 1932, national income went up to 71.2 billions in 1937; and after the recession of that year, national income was restored to 69.4 billions in 1939. But this did not bring the country back to where it had been before the depression had set in; the reasons were that the population had increased by ten millions in the decade since 1929 and that the productivity of the nation's industrial plants had also improved. That is to say, if the recovery had been complete and full use of the nation's manpower and resources had been made, the real income should have been in the neighborhood of at least 100 billions of dollars.

EFFECTS OF DEFICIT FINANCING. In another area the success of the New Deal's policy was only of mixed character. It has already been pointed out that the New Deal was spending large sums of money. Government bonds, bills, and notes for these sums flowed into the banks. The Board of Governors of the Federal Reserve System then followed a cheap money policy. They bought government bills and notes, and this led to an increase in the reserves of the member banks. Member bank reserves also grew through the inflow of gold from abroad. By these processes, the base of the credit pyramid was expanded. It was hoped that increased reserves would lead to increased bank deposits (as a result of commercial loans made by banks); and that increased deposits would lead to an expansion of employment and therefore greater spending.

But it did not work out that way. Deposits did grow because of government deficit financing. The banks, however, showed their increasing deposits in their investment portfolios rather than their loan portfolios. They were, in other words, maintaining themselves in an amazingly liquid form; and the first hint of contraction of business encouraged them to liquidate their loans and discounts. Also, government's unbalanced budget and its taxation of corporate profits, without making due allowances for losses, led to a growing conservatism on the part of businessmen as far as the inception of risk-taking enterprise was concerned. It may be said, very properly, that there was a strike of capital — but this was not due so much to political hostility as it was to the uncertainties and the fears possessing business. The New Deal, in other words, appeared to be incapable, by its fiscal policy, of restoring that confidence in the business community that was really the basis of a real revival.

The key to the New Deal successes was therefore this: it was to be found not nearly so much in new capital borrowings by business or in any real expansion in bank credit. It was due largely to deficit financing; and when New Deal spending slowed down — as happened from midsummer 1937 to late spring 1938 — then a real business recession set in. Only the resumption of a spending policy on the part of the New Deal made possible the revival of the summer of 1938. And the great war expenditures that began to appear with 1940 accounted for the impressive increases in industrial production and national income and for the elimination of unemployment.

The Cost of the New Deal

THE DEBT. What did all this cost? From 1930 on, the road of deficit financing had been pursued — the New Deal notably stepping up the tempo after 1933 — so that in the 1930s the federal debt was increased from about 16 billions of

dollars to more than 40 billions. During the first years of the decade, the deficits which the Federal government encountered resulted from a decline in receipts from tax sources, whereas, under the New Deal, they had resulted rather from an increase in expenditures. During the years 1931–1933 federal expenditures were in the neighborhood of 4 billions of dollars annually; in 1934 they were 6 billions, and in 1937, 8.4 billions. The New Deal insisted that the deficit was not entirely incurred because of "madework" activities. Thus for the years 1931–38 the total deficit was 20 billions. But against this amount were to be balanced assets arising from recoverable loans and expenditures on public-works construction; these came to 12 billions of dollars.

TAXES. At the same time that deficits increased, so did taxes. Federal taxes in 1931 came to 2.7 billions of dollars; in 1938 they stood at 5.9 billions. In 1931, federal taxes represented 4.5 percent of national income, whereas in 1938 the percentage was 9.5. Income-tax rates were pushed up; and in 1936, as a further tax on corporations, an undistributed-profits tax was levied. Because of the great hostility engendered, this device was abandoned in the Revenue Act of 1938. In 1930 at least 95 percent of all federal tax revenues were produced by income taxes, tobacco taxes, and customs duties; in 1938, these sources contributed 58 percent. The New Deal developed new tax sources, notably manufacturers' excise taxes, liquor taxes (because of repeal), and payroll taxes.

At the same time, it is important to note that the Federal government was not called upon to pay as much, proportionately, for its borrowings. The yield on United States government bonds was

3.65 percent in the second quarter of 1929 and only 2.7 percent in the last quarter of 1937.

Labor under the New Deal

In one sector there were real gains: organized labor grew, its rights were being safeguarded, and it was being paid better than ever before in its history. Too well, in fact, some authorities were prepared to argue. Interestingly enough, one of the important reasons for the extraordinary increase in trade-union membership (the other was the National Labor Relations Act) was the breaking out of a bitter internecine, schismatic dispute within the American Federation of Labor.

THE CIO. The leader of the schismatics was John L. Lewis, the ambitious and dynamic head of the United Mine Workers. The 1920s had seen a slackening of effort on the part of trade-union leaders. They had become involved in business investments, had frowned on social-security programs, and were incapable of coping with or indifferent to the great horde of the unorganized in the mass-production industries. One of the important reasons for this was that most union leaders were spokesmen for highly skilled craftsmen who were fearful of the inroads being made into their own special interests by the assembly-line technique. John L. Lewis did not belong in the company of these less alert leaders. He had taken advantage of Section 7(a) of the NIRA to press unionization in the coal industry. He was more sympathetic to the problems of the workers in the mass-production industries (steel, automobiles, rubber, oil refining, aluminum) because so many of his own members were more and more entering the class of semiskilled.

In any event, Mr. Lewis challenged the top leadership of the A. F. of L. at its 1935 convention when he forced a vote on a resolution demanding that organizational work be pushed on industrial lines in the basic industries instead of on craft lines. This meant that all men in the automobile industry, for example, were to be organized into an automobile union, instead of being unionized as machinists, teamsters, stationary engineers, and the like. Mr. Lewis was defeated, but he found enough support at the convention to encourage him to form the Committee for Industrial Organization within the A. F. of L. The CIO went ahead and, before 1936 was over, it had the backing of ten national and international unions, some of which had begun on their own account to do missionary work among the unorganized.

This led to open warfare. In 1936 the executive committee of the A. F. of L. suspended the ten unions that had joined the CIO; the next year the A. F. of L. convention authorized the expulsion of those unions which refused "to return to the ranks of our movement." Nine of the unions were so expelled in 1938, and the gage of battle was down. Lewis accepted it when he and his followers formally met in convention late in 1938 and, in November, set up the rival body of the Congress of Industrial Organizations. To a great extent the A. F. of L. clung to its basic role of organizing the skilled workers in craft unions, disregarding industrial groupings; while the CIO devoted itself to industrial unionism without paying attention to craft differences. But this did not prevent both bodies from cutting across the lines, so that a certain amount of dual unionism developed. What was profoundly significant was that the A. F. of L. became a fighting organization and explored the new opportunities for unionization as energetically as did the CIO. As a result, great gains were won by both, and when Pearl Harbor struck, each could claim at least 4,000,000 dues-paying members.

CIO SUCCESSES. The CIO's initial successes were unprecedented. It went into automobiles, revitalized the United Automobile Workers of America (which had been established in 1935), and challenged at once one of the greatest citadels of industrial power in the country, the General Motors Corporation. In December, 1936, strikes were called, and the sitdown (subsequently declared illegal) was used with telling effect. After forty days of bitter struggle, General Motors gave in and signed an agreement recognizing the union as the bargaining agency for its members in all the company's plants. The other automobile companies except Ford fell into line; even Ford capitulated in time. Next came steel, where a Steel Workers' Organizing Committee was formed, initially largely financed by the coal miners. Steel had been the hardest nut for trade unionism to crack as far back as 1892, when the disastrous Homestead Strike had destroyed the workers' organization. So completely did the SWOC do its work in the case of so-called Big Steel that in March, 1937, without a strike, the United States Steel Corporation signed an agreement much like that of the automobile industry. But the newer steel companies — they were called Little Steel and included the Republic Steel Corporation and the Bethlehem Steel Corporation — refused to yield, and bitter strikes swept the steel regions during May–July, 1937. Violence on both sides was common, with a good deal of vigilantism present. The stubborn resistance of the Little Steel leaders led to the failure of the strike in July. Other industrial areas where the CIO unions were successful were the Eastern maritime workers, the Western longshoremen, the rubber workers, and the aluminum workers.

A. F. OF L. AND CIO RIVALRY. Meanwhile, the rivalry between the A. F. of L. and CIO grew in intensity. Both engaged in mutual recriminations, the A. F. of L. being charged with giving haven to racketeers, and the CIO being charged with permitting communists to infiltrate its ranks. Both charges were true. The driving ambitions of John L. Lewis attracted general attention, and his interests and pretensions were frequently associated with the purposes of trade unionism in general. In the second Roosevelt administration his ardor toward the New Deal cooled and he openly broke with the President, supporting Wendell L. Willkie in 1940. His tactics estranged one of his best supporters, the International Ladies Garment Workers, and this union left the CIO and rejoined the A. F. of L. in 1940. Mr. Lewis found increasingly less support among CIO unions, and the personal bitterness that developed led to a strange move on his part. He withdrew from the CIO in 1942, and in 1943 made application for readmission to the A. F. of L.! In 1946, the miners were back in the fold again. The A. F. of L. continued under the leadership of William Green, and the CIO was now led by Philip Murray, who had been one of Lewis's vice presidents in the coal miners' union.

The possibility of fusion was remote, although it is important to note that the rivalry between the two bodies occupied relatively little of the energies of trade-union leaders. Trade unionism in the country went ahead on seven-league boots, in many industries obtaining virtually 100 percent membership and writing closed-shop agreements with increasing frequency. This, then, was one of the outstanding — if not the most ironical — achievements of the New Deal: it had made the American workers completely trade-union conscious and had converted them (except, perhaps, for the Australasians) into the most militant body of organized workers in the world. The trade unionists of the United States were not radical politically, only a small minority supporting a program of even mild state socialism; they were not entering politics as workers in their own parties; but they did fight constantly for improvement in working conditions. This was particularly true in connection with wage rates.

WAGES AND PRODUCTIVITY. Trade-union successes may have been too great as far as the effects on the total economy were concerned. Professor Sumner H. Slichter, for example, was able to argue that wage rates went up much more sharply than did productivity, the result being excessive additions to cost. This was likely to make the business enterpriser embarking on new ventures more cautious than he would ordinarily be. Professor Slichter pointed out that in the period 1921–26 physical productivity per man-hour in manufacturing increased 4.3 percent a year; in the period 1933–37 the increase was only 1.7 percent a year. Also, between 1921 and 1926, hourly earnings in manufacturing rose 8.4 percent; between 1933 and 1937, they rose 40 percent. Said Professor Slichter: "Physical productivity per man-hour grew twice as fast after 1921 as after 1933 or 1934, but wage rates went up twice as rapidly in the second period as in the first. These differences were not entirely compensated by price movements." And he came to this position: "For the time being, however, one must conclude that the spread of union-

ization tends to reduce the marginal return of capital."

The New Deal Continues in Power

THE CAMPAIGN OF 1936. The hostility to the New Deal, particularly as recovery continued on its uneven way, became more outspoken; but to organize this opposition was not easy. Nothing proved this more surely than the outcome of the presidential election of 1936. The Republicans had met first in June, 1936, and had come out flatly against the New Deal and all its works. Their platform opened with the words, "America is in peril," and in this spirit they submitted the principles and the achievements of the New Deal to a bitter arraignment. While there had been a good deal of preconvention scrambling for votes, there was no real opposition to the candidacy of Governor Alfred M. Landon of Kansas. He was named on the first ballot, and with him was nominated Frank Knox of Illinois for the vice presidency.

Mr. Roosevelt dominated the proceedings at the Democratic convention, although he did not appear in person. The New Deal was in a defiant mood because of Supreme Court hostility (the Court had found unconstitutional the NIRA and the AAA, among other measures) and the growing disapproval of the business community. It challenged both and pledged the administration to a continuing fight on "the activities of malefactors of great wealth who defraud and exploit the people." President Roosevelt and Vice President Garner were renominated by acclamation. Victory at the polls was achieved as easily. Labor flocked to the defense of the Democratic ticket, while the Republican cause was not aided by the support of those unreconstructed conservatives who refused to see that trade unionism and social security had come to stay. Landon, who was personally a liberal and sympathetic to many of the New Deal achievements, was put in an equivocal position and he never recovered. The President's reelection was one of the most impressive demonstrations of the popular will in American politics. He received a popular vote of 27,751,000 to Mr. Landon's 16,680,000, and he carried every state but Maine and Vermont.

THE SUPREME COURT FIGHT. Not only was Roosevelt's reelection a vote of confidence in the New Deal; it also put the stamp of approval on the President's fight against the Supreme Court. Or so he assumed. In any event, in February, 1937, there were sent to Congress a presidential message and a bill which called, in effect, for the packing of the bench. Justices might retire at the age of seventy; if they did not do so, the President had the right to appoint up to six additional members to supplement the nonretiring members. The storm that arose took the President by surprise. Party ranks were broken, old friends deserted ancient loyalties, and a bitter controversy raged in Congress and in the press for months. The President lost the support of his personal friend Governor Lehman of New York, and of Senator Wheeler of Montana, who had been one of the New Deal's most loyal defenders.

The backers of the President insisted that Congress was closer to the will of the people than the Court was. As Charles A. Beard put it: "Congress has the same right as the Supreme Court to be courageous and independent. If Congress . . . agrees with four of the Supreme Court Justices that five of the Justices have misread, misinterpreted, and in substance violated the Constitution, then Congress has the civic and moral obligation to bring the Court back within the

Constitution." The President's opponents, on the other hand, feared the destruction of the country's Constitutional liberties if the Supreme Court was compelled to become the rubber stamp of the Executive. The President entered the lists in person and made two public addresses in which he declared frankly that there was "no definite assurance that the three-horse team of the American system of government will pull together" and that he wanted "to appoint Justices who will not undertake to override Congress or legislative policy."

The President was unsuccessful because of the hostility of the Senate. His bill was reported out adversely by the Senate Judiciary Committee; a long debate ensued, and when his chief whip, Senator Robinson of Arkansas, died suddenly, the administration support collapsed. A substitute proposal was introduced and, because it pleased nobody, the Senate voted to recommit it on July 22. Thus the drama ended. For a short time, curiously enough, victory was with the President; for the withdrawal of three of his most persistent foes on the bench made it possible for him to appoint men who were more favorably disposed toward administration policies. Justice Van Devanter was succeeded by Senator Hugo Black of Alabama in 1937; Justice Sutherland was succeeded by Solicitor General Stanley Reed in 1938; and Justice Butler was succeeded by Attorney General Murphy in 1940. Now the Court began to talk with the tongue of the New Deal, and the President could say — as he did in one of his "fireside chats" in July, 1938 — that while he had lost a battle he had really won the war. But victory — especially in the long run — was with the Court too; for its independence and integrity had been preserved, and it survived as an independent agency to fight again another day if American liberties should be threatened.

SLOWING DOWN OF THE NEW DEAL. From this time on, the New Deal as domestic policy became less and less aggressive. For one thing, the President was meeting with more resistance in Congress, notably among those Southern legislators who were beginning to find their alliance with labor spokesmen an uneasy one. But more important, the President, after his "quarantine" speech at Chicago of October, 1937, was turning his attention almost completely to foreign affairs. He saw, as did Churchill in England, that Nazism was not a European program but a plan for world conquest, and he sought to awaken Americans to their peril. New Dealism was increasingly preoccupied with recovery questions; and here the chief weapons were the deficit financing of the Treasury and the control over banking policy of the Board of Governors of the Federal Reserve System. When the President, for example, sought to chastise those Congressmen and Senators who had failed to rally to him in the Supreme Court fight, by calling for their defeat in the elections of 1938, he was rebuffed by the electorate. The Republicans were beginning to creep up on the New Deal. In 1938 they elected governors in a number of states that had gone Democratic previously; and they won 80 seats in the House and 8 in the Senate. Cooperating with some 60 conservatives in the ranks of the Democracy, the Republicans were able to hold the more aggressive representatives of the New Deal in leash.

The Third-Term Election

Whether Roosevelt entertained thoughts of a third term before World War II broke out is hard to say. But one may note that by 1940, particularly after the collapse of France in May, it was apparent to him that our involvement was a matter of time alone. In fact, were Britain to fall, a victory for the Axis was clearly on the cards. The continuance, unbroken, of a foreign policy which stood for defiance to the Axis and aid to Britain preceded all other considerations. The Axis had to be defeated; and if this meant the shattering of the third-term tradition, that could not be helped. So, apparently, ran the President's thoughts and the thoughts of his consistent followers, notably those in the ranks of labor.

THE REPUBLICANS. The Republican delegates to the presidential nominating convention met at Philadelphia in June, 1940, in one of the most critical periods in American affairs. Division among Americans was quite as profound as it had been in the 1850s. Isolationists made light of the talk of our dangers at the hands of the Axis and were ready to accept the word of the Germans and the Japanese that the New Order was designed only for Europe, and the Co-Prosperity Sphere only for Eastern Asia. Interventionists were fearful, and they pointed not only to Hitler's military successes but also to the great victories gained by the Nazi ideology in our own midst and among the Latin American peoples. The Republicans were called upon to make a fateful choice. Interestingly enough, the choice was made not by the delegates but by the rank and file, who forced upon the convention the nomination of Wendell L. Willkie of Indiana and New York City. Willkie was named on the sixth ballot, and with him was nominated Senator McNary of Oregon.

Willkie was no standpatter; with much of the achievement of the New Deal he sympathized. He was opposed, however, to the New Deal's inefficiency and irresponsibility, to its hostility to business, and its willingness to build up a towering bureaucracy. On foreign policy he saw eye to eye with the President: Britain had to be aided, the Axis meant to fight us.

OUTCOME OF THE ELECTION OF 1940. Mr. Roosevelt said nothing about his successor to the Democratic convention at Chicago in July. While there was considerable opposition among party leaders to his being named, none came out into the open, and he was renominated on the first ballot. At his request, Secretary of Agriculture Henry A. Wallace was chosen as his running mate. The most important defection from the Democratic ranks was that of James A. Farley, who had nursed the President's political career throughout the long period of New York politics, and who had helped to elect him in 1932 and to reelect him in 1936. The charge of dictatorship had some effect on the voting; so did the issues of the European conflict as far as European-born peoples in our midst were concerned. The larger farmers of the Middle West returned to the Republican fold, and some of the professional and white-collar supporters of the earlier elections also dropped out of the Democratic ranks. But the President was triumphantly reelected, although by a reduced majority. Roosevelt's popular vote was 27,000,000 against Willkie's 22,000,000; his electoral vote 449 against Willkie's 82. The Republicans carried ten New England and Midwestern states — and that was all.

The New Deal and the Problem of Bureaucracy

There was no doubt that the New Deal had come to grips with a series of important and pressing problems. From the social point of view, its accomplishment had been significant: it had sought to end insecurity and it had helped the American labor movement to mature. From the economic point of view, its programs had resulted in the raising of quite as many questions as it had sought to answer. It was in the political sector, however, that New Deal planning had stepped out boldly into the unknown; with what consequences to the traditional American way of life it was hard to measure.

CHARACTER OF STATE INTERVENTIONISM. For the New Deal had parted completely with the nineteenth century conception of the laissez-faire, or passive, state; Americans were fully launched on the experiment of state capitalism. The depression of 1930 and after had persuaded New Deal theoreticians that capitalism's progress in the United States had slowed down, if it had not ceased altogether. Now the state had to assume positive functions. Accordingly, its role as umpire was magnified and extended into other regions —as in the case of the establishment of the National Labor Relations Board and the Securities and Exchange Commission. Its social-service functions were expanded, particularly in the handling of the problems of the unemployed, the unemployables, and other dependents.

Nor was this all. Under the New Deal the state began to initiate projects and undertakings of a distinctly economic character. The national state, in short, was beginning to take on, in many domains, the essential color of private enterprise. It borrowed money, not alone for the maintenance of the traditional civil and military establishments of government, but also for the purposes of buying and selling commodities, processing goods, creating electric power and light, dealing in real estate, engaging in warehousing, the banking business, and the shipping and railroading businesses. It set up corporations and corporate agencies which possessed charters, directors, assets, thousands of employees, and industrial and mercantile policies. As in big business, there were interlocking directorates and the shifting of funds.

PROBLEMS RAISED BY STATISM. This was a startling transformation; and it raised for many Americans disquieting problems. There were — even before our entry into World War II — at least fifty such New Deal corporations and corporate agencies which were in or could go into business. Some were created by Congress, some by presidential order, some by departmental decision alone. Often they were run by Cabinet officers who, in the nature of things, were compelled to delegate power to anonymous lesser officials. The pattern was too complex and too obscure for popular control.

To whom, in the final analysis, were these executive agencies to be responsible? To Congress? But Congress did not possess any longer a machinery sensitive enough for their surveillance. Its committee system had been laid out for a simpler day; and to keep track of all the executive agencies would require a functionary group quite as complex as that already managing the new authorities and offices. By what tests was the worth of these new public bodies to be measured? By those of private business? But the New Deal authorities and offices did not have to enter the money market for fresh funds; they did not have to conserve assets; they were not called upon to present favorable profit-and-loss statements. Wage policies were fixed by statute and not by the competition of the market place.

How — most important of all — were the functionaries to be prevented from extending their authority? For here lay the real danger of a bureaucracy: that it tended to associate its own well-being with the general welfare. This was one of the vexing problems the New Deal had

created. It was not possible to dismiss it lightly or to seek to disguise its perils by referring to the new state as the "social-service state." Even as the war progressed, the question of this new American bureaucracy could not be downed, and it was one of the important reasons for the increasingly critical tone that Congress took toward the President.

During the later years of the Roosevelt administration, however, these critical questions were latent, if not far below the surface. The country's response to unrest abroad was absorbing more and more the attention of all parties.

International Relations under the
New Deal

Up to October, 1937 — always excepting the Good Neighbor policy and Secretary of State Hull's reciprocal trading program — the New Deal's foreign policy had a definitely nationalistic orientation. Economic revival in the rest of the world apparently was not to be a direct concern of the United States; if America could reestablish high levels of employment and increase its national income, then our prosperity would flow out beyond our shores and in time cover the whole earth. That we had become fully integrated into world affairs politically and economically — and that we could not pull ourselves up by our own bootstraps — were ideas only dimly felt in Washington.

An American delegation was sent to London in June, 1933, to attend the World Economic Conference, which was to concern itself with the stabilization of currencies, the freeing of the flow of world trade, and international prices. And then suddenly by Roosevelt's order — and to the dismay of Europeans generally — the Americans refused to tie their currency to that of the British or promise to defend the gold standard. The conference ended in failure.

Congress showed no greater wisdom. In April, 1934, it passed the Johnson Act. Under this, those nations which had received loans from the American government during World War I and which after 1930 had defaulted on interest payments were denied the right to float public securities in the American money market. Thus American capital resources were not to be made available to the European powers for the purposes of assisting them in coming to grips with their own economic difficulties; or indeed in helping them obtain funds here for rearmament purposes after 1936, when the menace of Hitler had become very real.

THE GOOD NEIGHBOR POLICY. In our relations with the countries of the Western Hemisphere we were more farsighted. As has been pointed out, a good beginning had been made by Secretaries of State Kellogg and Stimson during 1927–33. Roosevelt, with the assistance of Secretary of State Cordell Hull, happily continued along these paths. In his First Inaugural, Roosevelt had defined the Good Neighbor as one who "resolutely respects himself, and because he does so, respects the rights of others — the neighbor who respects his obligations and respects the sanctity of his agreements in and with a world of neighbors."

When revolution broke out in Cuba, Roosevelt not only refused to intervene, but he also offered and sent American economic assistance to the distressed republic. In 1934, the new government of Cuba was recognized; and a few months later, our protectorate was terminated by the repeal of the Platt Amendment. The same summer saw the recall of American marines from Haiti; and in 1935, the United States relinquished its financial control over the Haitian government. Also in 1935, cooperating with Latin American governments, the United States succeeded in terminating the war between Chile and Paraguay; and in 1936 our treaty rights in Panama were given up and that little republic was now truly independent for the first time.

In January, 1936, Roosevelt appeared in person at the Pan American conference being held at Buenos Aires — he was the first President of the United States ever to have visited South America while in office — and gave further pledges of his devotion to the idea of the Good Neighbor. A consultative pact was signed under which the signatories pledged to consult together in the event of war or intervention in the Western Hemisphere. The United States was moving toward converting the Good Neighbor policy into a mutilateral understanding.

This, in fact, was achieved in 1940 at the Havana Conference when the so-called Act of Havana was drawn up. The Act of Havana was prefaced by the statement that "the status of regions in this continent belonging to European Powers is a subject of deep concern to all the governments of the American Republics." And then the Act went on to pledge all the signatories to regard as an aggressive measure against all of them "any attempt on the part of a non-American State against the integrity or inviolability of the territory, the sovereignty, or the political independence of an American State." It is true that the Monroe Doctrine continued to be stated as an American unilateral declaration; but the Act of Havana reaffirmed it in multilateral terms. To this degree, therefore, the Latin American nations were prepared to accept the pledge of the United States that the Monroe Doctrine was directed against non-American Powers entirely.

RECIPROCAL TRADE AGREEMENTS. The Reciprocal Trade Agreements Act of 1934 gave the President power to conclude with other countries conventions under which tariff rates could be reduced as much as 50 percent — all this without the need for calling upon Congress to approve. There was only one safeguard included in the act: no item was to be added to or taken from the free list. Under the law, the State Department was to draw up the agreements, being assisted in these activities by a series of interdepartmental committees headed by experts. Public hearings were to be held, in order to afford proper protection for the interests of American business groups. The most-favored nation idea was also provided for, so that concessions granted to one country would apply to all countries that did not discriminate against us. Thus the benefits of revision downward would spread out in widening circles, including not only those nations which signed agreements with us but also those nations with whom signatories of the American acts were writing new agreements.

By 1937, when the act was renewed for another three years, agreements had already been written with fourteen countries. These covered more than a third of our total foreign trade, and they had the effect of increasing foreign trade with the signatory nations more than 40 percent. America's tariff wall was still high; but, at least, we were showing good faith in our desire to break down barriers to free exchanges the world over. Congress continued to renew the Trade Agreements Act in the 1930s and 1940s.

THE NEUTRALITY ACTS. Despite these manifestations of an interest in the world outside our shores, the prevailing American temper was isolationist. Nothing demonstrated this better than the Neutrality Acts of 1935, 1936, and 1937. As a result of the investigations of the Senate Munitions Committee, headed by Gerald P. Nye of North Dakota, Congress and a good part of the American people had become convinced that the munition makers had in very considerable measure been responsible for the entrance of the United States into World War I. To prevent our involvement in new international conflicts, therefore, Congress passed the first of its Neutrality Laws in August, 1935. This provided that upon the outbreak of war, an embargo was to be imposed by the President upon the export of implements of war; also, at his discretion, he might prohibit Americans from traveling on the ships of belligerent nations except at their own risk. The act was to be in force until February, 1936.

The second Neutrality Act — the joint resolution of February, 1936, which was to apply until May, 1937 — further cut down the area of presidential discretionary action. In 1935, Italy had invaded Ethiopia, and Americans saw the League of Nations struggling ineffectively against this act of aggression. They were sure, therefore, they were on the right course; we must not be drawn into the troubles of Europe at any price. The second act, therefore, preserved the mandatory embargo on implements of war and permitted the President to extend it to other exports. Belligerent powers were to be denied the right to raise funds in American money markets.

Between the second and the third neutrality acts, civil war broke out in Spain; Italy, Germany, and Russia intervened; and the Berlin-Rome Axis was established. There was no doubt that an international conflict was impending. In such a climate, with the isolationists still in the saddle, the third Neutrality Act — the joint resolution of May 1, 1937 — was drawn up. Unlike its predecessors, this was to be a permanent commitment. It continued the mandatory embargo on arms, munitions, and implements of war and the prohibition on credits to belligerents. It denied Americans the right to travel on ships of belligerents under any circumstances. It refused to allow American merchant ships to arm. And, for two years, all goods destined for nations at war were to come under the "cash and carry" provision: they were to be carried away in non-American ships and they were to be paid for before they left the country.

THE QUARANTINE ADDRESS. Up to this time, Roosevelt's own attitude toward the disorders beginning to appear throughout the world remained unclear. So, in January, 1936, he was prepared to accept all the terms of the first Neutrality Act. Again, to the chagrin of many American liberals, it was the President himself who asked Congress in January, 1937, to impose an arms embargo on Spain — and this despite the fact that the duly constituted Loyalist government was being fought by insurgents openly supported by Italy and Germany. Further, in order to apply the arms embargo to the Italo-Ethiopian conflict, the President had declared a state of war in existence before diplomatic relations between the two countries had even been suspended. And on the other hand, he had refused to recognize a state of war in China, even after Japanese aggression had become unmasked, as early as 1931.

By 1936, it was apparent that Japan was ready to cut herself free from all international commitments. In January of that year, the Japanese delegation quit the naval conference in London because the other Powers would not grant Japan parity; this meant the denunciation of the London Naval Treaty of 1930 and the resumption of capital ship construction. And in November, Japan signed the Anti-Comintern Pact: it had taken its stand beside the other two aggressors, Germany and Italy.

In July, 1937, the Japanese launched their full-scale offensive against the Chinese, when the Marco Polo Bridge incident opened hostilities. Before the year was over, without the formal declaration of war, Japan had extended its military operations over a good part of northern and central China. The Japanese poured armies into that unhappy country and engaged in atrocities against civilian populations.

One such was the general aerial bombing of the populous city of Nanking. It was after this attack that President Roosevelt came to understand that America no longer could remain an onlooker as the flames of war crept over the world. In Chicago on October 5, he delivered his famous Quarantine Address in which he called the attention of the American people to the fact that Japanese, German, and Italian aggression was imperilling our safety. And he issued this portentous warning to his fellow countrymen:

Let no one imagine that America will escape, that America may expect mercy, that this Western Hemisphere will not be attacked and that it will continue tranquilly and peacefully to carry on the ethics and the arts of civilization. . . . If we are to have a world in which we can breathe freely and live in amity without fear, the peace-loving nations must make a concerted effort to uphold laws and principles on which peace can rest secure. . . .

President Roosevelt declared boldly, therefore, that he would quarantine aggressors. From that day to the attack on Pearl Harbor, the administration left no stone unturned to prepare the United States against future eventualities.

PREPAREDNESS. In January, 1938, the President called Congress' attention to the fact that other nations were rearming; and he asked for new naval construction. Congress quickly complied and passed the administration measure much as the naval experts had drawn it up. The Naval Act of 1938 authorized the expenditure of more than a billion dollars on new capital ships, airplane carriers, and cruisers; the United States was beginning to move toward the development of that two-ocean navy which alone could defend the two seas on which it faced.

Meanwhile, relations with Japan were steadily deteriorating. In December, 1937, Japanese aircraft bombed and destroyed the American gunboat *Panay* on the Yangtsze River. It is true that the Japanese made immediate apologies and offered indemnification; but the State Department refused to assume that this was to be the last of the unfriendly acts of the Japanese toward the United States.

Checking Japanese aggression was not an easy matter, however. And America's position was becoming increasingly difficult as the European Powers themselves found no formulas to preserve peace. In September, 1938, England and France abandoned Czechoslovakia to its fate when they surrendered the Sudetenland to Hitler at Munich. In March, 1939, Hitler marched into Czechoslovakia with none to gainsay him; in the same month he took Memel. In April, Mussolini seized Albania. France and England knew that Poland was to be the next victim, and they declared unequivocally that they would fight if Hitler moved eastward. But Hitler was wiser than they assumed; he was not ready — yet — to wage a two-front war. He proceeded to assure his safety on the east by the German-Soviet Pact of August 22, 1939. On September 1, the German armies were in Poland and World War II had commenced.

Poland quickly fell while the French army sat behind the safety — so it believed — of the Maginot Line. And then, after they had exploited fully the psychological effects of the so-called "phony war" in the west, the German armies swung across the Rhine into the Low Countries and France. France, unprepared and badly led, fell in June, 1940. Only England stood out against the successful German Wehrmacht. And in September, 1940, Japan, Germany, and Italy signed the Tripartite Pact, which bound them together in a military alliance.

Only now did America begin to put its house in order. The navy was granted further appropriations; the President was given the right to call out the National Guard; in September, the Selective Service Act was passed. To protect us from surprise attacks — and to help England — in the same month we released fifty over-age destroyers to the British navy in exchange for long-term leases in British possessions in the Western Hemisphere where we could build air and naval bases. Our vigilance toward the Japanese also was commendable. In July, 1940 — to check the flow of vital war materials eastward — the Export Control Act gave the President power to curtail or prohibit the movement of such goods. Licenses were refused for the export of aviation gasoline and most types of machine tools. In October, the export of iron and steel scrap to Japan was embargoed.

Then, we committed ourselves. For, in March, 1941, Congress passed the Lend-Lease Act — and we were launched, as Roosevelt said, upon a "policy of unqualified, immediate, all-out aid for Britain, Greece, China, and for all the governments in exile whose homelands are temporarily occupied by the aggressors." An undeclared naval war broke out in the Atlantic; but Japan and not Hitler struck first.

PEARL HARBOR. On June 22, 1941, without warning, Germany attacked Russia; and at the same time Japanese pretensions toward the whole of southeastern Asia were revealed. It was evident to America that Japan was preparing for a large-scale offensive that threatened not only French Indo-China (which indeed it had already occupied), but also Malaya, Burma, and the Netherlands Indies. We warned the Japanese against such moves; and for a time they temporized. They sent a new ambassador, Admiral Nomura, to Washington and he and Secretary Hull carried on discussions during the greater part of 1941. In November, Nomura was joined by a special emissary, Saburo Kurusu; there were further conversations, with Roosevelt and Hull both participating in them — but no agreements were reached. Meanwhile General Tojo, an open warmonger, had become the Japanese prime minister; and it was plain to American Ambassador Grew at Tokyo that Japan meant to fight. Washington was warned accordingly, and members of the administration, in public addresses, began to prepare the American people for hostilities.

The attack came from an unexpected quarter. Early Sunday morning, December 7, the Japanese struck at Pearl Harbor from the air. The next day, President Roosevelt appeared before Congress and asked for the declaration of a state of war. Congress complied at once, there being but one dissenting vote. Three days later, Germany and Italy declared war on the United States.

The United States was in World War II. It was committed to the destruction of the Axis Powers and to the termination of the threat of aggression everywhere. After more than twenty years, America had returned to take its place in that "one world" which it had mistakenly assumed it could disregard. American prosperity and security were linked with welfare and peace everywhere on the face of the earth. To this point the Third American Revolution had brought the American people, some three and one-half centuries after Elizabethan England had begun to dream of establishing settlements on the North American mainland.

Henry Steele Commager:

TWELVE YEARS OF ROOSEVELT

NOW that the bitter controversies over New Deal policies have been drowned out by the clamor of war, it is possible to evaluate those policies in some historical perspective. And now that the outcome of this war which is to determine the future of democracy and of America's rôle in world affairs, is certain, it is possible to interpret something of the significance of the foreign policy, or program, of the Roosevelt administrations. Those policies, domestic and foreign, have been four times decisively endorsed by large popular majorities: so fully have they been translated into accomplished and irrevocable facts that controversy about them is almost irrelevant. It should be possible to fix, if not with finality, at least with some degree of accuracy, the place occupied by Roosevelt in American history.

That this place still seems clouded by controversy and bitterness cannot be denied. Yet this, too, is part of the picture and has its own significance. The Washington, the Jefferson, the Jackson, the Lincoln, the Wilson administrations, too, were characterized by controversy and bitterness; it is only the administrations of mediocre men like Monroe, Arthur, Harrison, that are memorable for placidity. The explanation of the controversy and especially of the bitterness is, however, less rational. It is a two-fold one: contemporaries tended to see in both the domestic and foreign policies of Roosevelt an abrupt and even revolutionary break with the past; they tended to personalize those policies, to regard them as largely an expression of Roosevelt's character, to focus all their attention — both their devotion and their hatred — on the man in the White House rather than on the groundswell of opinion to which he gave expression.

We can see now that the "Roosevelt revolution" was no revolution, but rather the culmination of half a century of historical development, and that Roosevelt himself, though indubitably a leader, was an instrument of the popular will rather than a creator of, or a dictator to, that will. Indeed, the two major issues of the Roosevelt administration — the domestic issue of the extension of government control for democratic purposes, and the international issue of the rôle of America as a world power — emerged in the 1890's, and a longer perspective will see the half-century from the 1890's to the present as an historical unit. The roots of the New Deal, the origins of our participation in this war, go deep down into our past, and neither development is comprehensible except in terms of that past.

What was really but a new deal of the old cards looked, to startled and dismayed contemporaries, like a revolution for two reasons: because it was carried through with such breathless rapidity,

From the *American Mercury*, 60 (April, 1945), 391–401, by permission of the publisher.

and because in spirit at least it contrasted so sharply with what immediately preceded. But had the comparison been made not with the Coolidge-Hoover era, but with the Wilson, the Theodore Roosevelt, even the Bryan era the contrast would have been less striking than the similarities. Actually, precedent for the major part of New Deal legislation was to be found in these earlier periods. Regulation of railroads and of business dated back to the Interstate Commerce Act of 1887 and the Sherman Act of 1890, and was continuous from that time forward. The farm relief program of the Populists, and of Wilson, anticipated much that the Roosevelt administrations enacted. The beginnings of conservation can be traced to the Carey Act of 1894 and the Reclamation Act of 1902, and the first Roosevelt did as much as the second to dramatize — though less to solve — the program of conserving natural resources.

Power regulation began with the Water Power Act of 1920; supervision over securities exchanges with grain and commodities exchange acts of the Harding and Coolidge administrations; while regulation of money is as old as the Union, and the fight which Bryan and Wilson waged against the "Money Power" and Wall Street was more bitter than anything that came during the New Deal. The policy of reciprocity can be traced to the Republicans, Blaine and McKinley. Labor legislation had its beginnings in such states as Massachusetts and New York over half a century ago, while much of the program of social security was worked out in Wisconsin and other states during the second and the third decades of the new century.

There is nothing remarkable about this, nor does it detract in any way from the significance of President Roosevelt's achievements and contributions. The pendulum of American history swings gently from right to left, but there are no sharp breaks in the rhythm of our historical development; and it is to the credit of Roosevelt that he worked within the framework of American history and tradition.

2

What, then, are the major achievements, the lasting contributions, of the first three Roosevelt administrations? First, perhaps, comes the restoration of self-confidence, the revivification of the national spirit, the reassertion of faith in democracy. It is irrelevant to argue whether these things were achieved by Roosevelt, or whether they came, rather, as a result of extraneous forces — as needless as to argue whether Jackson really was concerned with the rise of the common man, or Lincoln with abolition, or the first Roosevelt with reform. These things are irrevocably associated with their administrations, and it is safe to prophesy that the revival of faith in democracy, after a long decade of materialism and cynicism, will be associated with Franklin Roosevelt.

More, a strong case can be made out for the propriety of that association. "The only thing we need to fear," said Mr. Roosevelt on assuming the Presidency, "is fear itself. . . . We face the arduous days that lie before us in the warm courage of national unity; with the clear consciousness of seeking old and precious moral values; with the clean satisfaction that comes from the stern performance of duty." And during twelve years of office, Mr. Roosevelt did not abate his confidence in "the future of essential democracy" or in the capacity of the American people to rise to any challenge, to meet any crisis, domestic or foreign. Those who lived through the electric spring of 1933 will remember the change from depression and discouragement to excitement and hope; those able to compare the last decade with previous decades will agree that interest in public affairs has rarely been as widespread, as alert, or as responsive.

All this may be in the realm of the intangible. If we look to more tangible things, what does the record show? Of primary importance has been the physical rehabilitation of the country. Notwithstanding the splendid achievements of the Theodore Roosevelt administrations, it became clear, during the twenties and thirties, that the natural resources of the country — its soil, forests, water power — were being destroyed at a dangerous rate. The development of the Dust Bowl, and the migration of the Oakies to the Promised Land of California, the tragic floods on the Mississippi and the Ohio, dramatized to the American people the urgency of this problem.

Roosevelt tackled it with energy and boldness. The Civilian Conservation Corps enlisted almost three million young men who planted seventeen million acres in new forests, built over six million check dams to halt soil erosion, fought forest fires and plant and animal diseases. To check erosion the government organized a co-operative program which enlisted the help of over one-fourth the farmers of the country and embraced 270 million acres of land, provided for the construction of a series of huge dams and reservoirs, and planned the creation of a hundred-mile-wide shelter belt of trees on the high plains. The Resettlement Administration moved farmers off marginal lands and undertook to restore these to usefulness. More important than all this, was the TVA, a gigantic laboratory for regional reconstruction. Though much of this program owes its inspiration to the past, the contrast between the New

Deal and what immediately preceded it cannot be better illustrated than by reference to Hoover's characterization of the Muscle Shoals bill of 1931 as not "liberalism" but "degeneration."

Equally important has been the New Deal achievement in the realm of human rehabilitation. Coming into office at a time when unemployment had reached perhaps fourteen million, and when private panaceas had ostentatiously failed, it was perhaps inevitable that Roosevelt should have sponsored a broad program of government aid. More important than bare relief, was the acceptance of the principle of the responsibility of the state for the welfare and security of its people — for employment, health and general welfare.

That this principle was aggressively and bitterly opposed now seems hard to believe: its establishment must stand as one of the cardinal achievements of the New Deal. Beginning with emergency legislation for relief, the Roosevelt program in the end embraced the whole field of social security — unemployment assistance, old age pensions, aid to women and children, and public health. Nor did it stop with formal "social security" legislation. It entered the domains of agriculture and labor, embraced elaborate programs of rural rehabilitation, the establishment of maximum hours and minimum wages, the prohibition of child labor, housing reform, and, eventually, enlarged aid to education. Under the New Deal the noble term "commonwealth" was given a more realistic meaning than ever before in our history.

That to Roosevelt the preservation of democracy was closely associated with this program for social and economic security is inescapably clear. He had learned well the moral of recent continental European history: that given a choice between liberty and bread, men are sorely tempted to choose bread. The task of democracy, as he conceived it, was to assure both. In a fireside chat of 1938 he said:

Democracy has disappeared in several other great nations, not because the people of those nations disliked democracy, but because they had grown tired of unemployment and insecurity, of seeing their children hungry while they sat helpless in the face of government confusion and government weakness through lack of leadership in government. Finally, in desperation, they chose to sacrifice liberty in the hope of getting something to eat. We in America know that our democratic institutions can be preserved and made to work. But in order to preserve them we need . . . to prove that the practical operation of democratic government is equal to the task of protecting the security of the people. . . . The people of America are in agreement in defending their liberties at any cost, and the first line of that defense lies in the protection of economic security.

3

In the political realm the achievements of the New Deal were equally notable. First we must note the steady trend towards the strengthening of government and the expansion of government activities — whether for weal or for woe only the future can tell. As yet no better method of dealing with the crowding problems of modern economy and society has revealed itself, and it can be said that though government today has, quantitatively, far greater responsibilities than it had a generation or even a decade ago, it has, qualitatively, no greater power. For our Constitutional system is intact, and all power still resides in the people and their representatives in Congress, who can at any moment deprive their government of any power.

But we seem to have solved, in this country, the ancient problem of the reconciliation of liberty and order; we seem to have overcome our traditional distrust of the state and come to a realization that a strong state could be used to benefit and advance the commonwealth. That is by no means a New Deal achievement, but it is a development which has gained much from the experience of the American people with their government during the Roosevelt administrations.

It has meant, of course, a marked acceleration of the tendency towards Federal centralization. This tendency had been under way for a long time before Roosevelt came to office: a century ago liberals were deploring the decline of the states and the growth of the power of the national government. That under the impact first of depression and then of war it has proceeded at a rapid rate since 1933 cannot be denied. It is apparent in the administrative field, with the growth of bureaus and departments and civil servants — and of the budget! It is apparent in the legislative field, with the striking extension of Federal authority into the fields of labor, agriculture, banking, health, education and the arts. It is apparent in the executive field with the immense increase in the power of the President. And it has been ratified by the judiciary with the acceptance and application of a broad construction of the Constitution.

Yet it cannot be said that this Federal centralization has weakened the states or local communities. What we are witnessing is a general increase in governmental activities — an increase in which the states share — witness any state budget at present. And it can be argued, too, that political centralization strengthens rather than weakens local government and the health of local communities. For if we look below forms to realities we can see that during the last decade Federal aid to farmers, to home-owners, to labor, Federal assistance in road-building, education and public health, has actually restored many communities to financial and economic health. It is by no means certain that community sentiment is weaker today than it was a generation ago.

Along with Federal centralization has gone a great increase in the power of the executive. The charge that Roosevelt has been a dictator can be dismissed, along with those hoary charges that Jefferson, Jackson, Lincoln, Theodore Roosevelt, and Wilson were dictators. American politics simply doesn't run to dictators. But Roosevelt has been a "strong" executive — as every great democratic President has been a strong executive. There is little doubt that the growing complexity of government plays into the hands of the executive; there is little doubt that Roosevelt accepted this situation cheerfully. Today Roosevelt exercises powers far vaster than those contemplated by the Fathers of the Constitution, as vast, indeed, as those exercised by the head of any democratic state in the world. Yet it cannot fairly be asserted that any of these powers has been exercised arbitrarily, or that the liberties of Americans are not so safe today as at any other time.

Two other political developments under the New Deal should be noted. The first is the revitalization of political parties; the second the return of the Supreme Court to the great tradition of Marshall, Story, Miller and Holmes. For observations about political parties during the last decade are in order. First, the danger that our parties might come to represent a particular class or section or interest

was avoided: both major parties retained — after the election of 1936 — a broad national basis. Second, minor parties all but disappeared: in the elections of 1940 and 1944 the minor parties cast less than 1 per cent of the total vote — the first time this happened since 1872. Third, legislation such as the Hatch Act diminished the possibility that any party might come to be controlled by powerful vested interests or by patronage. And finally, with the organization of the PAC in the campaign of 1944, labor for the first time in our history became an important factor in elections; and labor chose to work within the framework of existing parties rather than, as elsewhere, to organize its own party.

The New Deal, as far as can be foreseen, is here to stay: there seems no likelihood of a reversal of any of the major developments in politics in the last twelve years. This was recognized by the Republicans in 1940 and again in 1944, for both platforms endorsed all the essentials of the New Deal and confined criticism to details and administration. How far the reforms and experiments of the Roosevelt era will be carried is a hazardous question. That the program of conservation will be continued and enlarged seems obvious. A recent Congress, to be sure, cavalierly ended the life of the National Resources Planning Board, but the present Congress seems disposed to undertake a Missouri Valley development along the lines of the TVA, and doubtless other "little TVA's" are ahead. Social security, too, will be maintained and possibly enlarged: whether it will come to embrace socialized medicine or a broad rehousing program is more dubious.

There may be a reaction against some of the labor legislation of the New Deal, but labor's newly discovered political power would seem to make that unlikely. It is improbable that there will be any relaxation of governmental peacetime controls over business, banking, securities, power, though here a change in taxation policies may do much to stimulate private enterprise and create an appearance of a shift away from New Deal practices. Federal centralization, which has been under way so long, is doubtless here to stay; planning, imperatively required by war, will in all probability wear off its faintly pink tinge, and flourish as a peacetime technique. And, finally, it seems probable that the restoration of the dignity of politics and statecraft, which came with 1933, will survive.

Today it is foreign affairs rather than domestic policy that commands our most agitated attention. Here, too, the large outlines of the Roosevelt achievements are clear, though the details are blurred and the future projection uncertain.

4

The problem of America's rôle in world affairs has been with us in one form or another since Colonial days. Then, we are sometimes inclined to forget, we were heavily involved in the affairs of the Western world — but as victims, one might say, rather than as independent participants. Our War for Independence was a world war; our War of 1812 was part of another world war. Between 1815 and the 1890's we achieved, or fancied that we achieved, some degree of isolation, but for two out of three centuries of our history we have been inextricably entangled in world affairs. In the 1890's we aggressively assumed a position as a world power, and the roots of our present involvement trace back to that decade. It is unnecessary to rehearse the details of that emergence as a world

power: the Spanish War, the acquisition of Hawaii and of the Philippines, the Open Door policy, the reassertion of the Monroe Doctrine and the addition of corollaries, the construction of a powerful navy, indirect participation in the Algeciras Conference and intervention to end the Russo-Japanese War. All these and other indications dramatized the fact that the United States was a world power, with world-wide interests.

Since that time isolation has been a delusion. How futile that delusion was, was revealed by our participation in the first World War; how profound and widespread it was, was confessed in the retreat of the twenties — the refusal to join the League or the World Court, the withdrawal from the Far East, the gestures towards economic self-sufficiency, the adolescent disillusionment with the world.

Reflected on the background of a half-century of experience, Roosevelt's understanding of the responsibility of America as a world power seems logical and obvious; contrasted with the half-baked and half-witted isolationism of the twenties it becomes not only creditable but impressive. The international problems of the thirties were at once more complex and more urgent than those of any previous decade.

Future generations may indeed wonder that Americans of the thirties could have been paralyzed by hesitation and doubt, and may find in the neutrality legislation of 1935–37 one of the most intriguing enigmas of history; the historian can but record that opinion was divided, that the majority seemed to approve of this legislation, and that this majority included its share of the intelligent and the sincere.

We know now that from the time Japan struck in Manchuria and Hitler entered the Rhineland the issue confronting the United States was one of ultimate survival. It is to the credit of President Roosevelt that he sensed this from the beginning, that his record of hostility to what Hitler represented is clear and consistent, and that from 1937 on he sought ceaselessly to rally American opinion against totalitarianism and to prepare America for the test that finally came.

Campaign orators have lamented that he was not more outspoken than he was, that he did not take more aggressive steps, make more energetic preparations. These critics conveniently forgot that Roosevelt was consistently ahead of public opinion — witness the reaction to the Quarantine speech of 1937 — and that in a democracy public opinion is the ultimate tribunal to which even a President must bow. And those who think that America was inexcusably unready for war in December 1941 should compare our readiness then with our pitiful state of unreadiness in April 1917 — after almost three years of warning.

5

Roosevelt's foreign policy has, indeed, over a period of twelve years, a remarkable consistency — a consistency sometimes concealed from us by specific and minor aberrations. From the beginning he worked within the framework of the American system and respected the limitations of American politics. He did not attempt to reopen the issue of the League; he conceded defeat on the issue of the World Court; he accepted — though as we now know reluctantly — neutrality legislation. With reference to the European and Pacific problem he did what he could. He kept the record straight, insisted upon the validity of the

principles involved, educated the American people to the underlying issues, set our domestic house in order, and pushed forward a naval building program. When the test came, there was much still to be done; there was nothing to retract.

From 1939 on, both the material and the moral achievements were of inestimable importance. On the material side the achievement was spectacular. There was the destroyer-bases deal which at once strengthened Britain in her heroic struggle against the Nazis and America in her self-defense. There was the Lend-Lease program which made America a veritable arsenal of democracy and which may eventually be regarded as the decisive turning point of the war. There was the acquisition of bases in Greenland and Iceland, and the "shoot on sight" order against German U-boats. There was the first peacetime conscription — the continuation of which was saved by a single vote in the lower House. There was the development of a vast and marvelously organized program of industrial mobilization — shipbuilding, munitions manufacture, airplane production. Without all this, it is safe to say the war would have been lost.

The moral achievement will probably be better appreciated by future generations than by our own. Like Wilson, Roosevelt put the issues at once upon a moral plane, and kept them there: without Wilson's eloquence, Roosevelt had fundamentally the same philosophy — a philosophy fundamentally religious and moral. If the Atlantic Charter seems tarnished at the moment, we must remember that the Fourteen Points, too, came to seem tarnished. The tarnish rubs off. Roosevelt made clear, from the beginning, that this was more than a war for self-defense, a task which the Germans and Japanese made relatively easy for him. In a war message reminiscent of Wilson's he declared that

the true goal we seek is far above and beyond the ugly field of battle. When we resort to force, as now we must, we are determined that this force shall be directed toward ultimate good as well as against immediate evil. We Americans are not destroyers — we are builders. . . . And in the dark hours of this day — and through dark days that may be yet to come — we will know that the vast majority of the members of the human race are on our side. Many of them are fighting with us. All of them are praying for us. For, in representing our case, we represent theirs as well — our hope and their hope for liberty under God.

When war finally came, the nation was united — united as it had never been for any previous war. That the war has been fought with effectiveness and efficiency cannot be doubted: compared with any previous war in which our unmilitary people have been involved, compared even with World War I, this has been a very miracle of efficiency. The details need not detain us; the results are sufficient.

Yet one more observation needs to be made with respect to Roosevelt's foreign policy, and that has to do with his comprehension of the problems of the future. Like Wilson, Roosevelt has envisioned a postwar international organization empowered to maintain peace. He has, so far, managed to avoid most of the errors which helped defeat Wilson's plans. Instead of keeping aloof from our Allies, he has associated with them, thus laying the groundwork now for a group of united nations. Instead of postponing the practical details of international co-operation, he has sponsored a series of conferences — relief, currency, aviation, Dumbarton

Oaks — looking to the creation, now, of machinery competent to the solution of the most pressing problems. Instead of regarding Russia as a menace or a broken reed, he has actively and enthusiastically co-operated with her. Instead of antagonizing the Senate, he has taken the Senate and the American people into his confidence. Many problems still confront us and plague us, but that the outlook for an effective international order is more auspicious now than at any previous time in our history can scarcely be denied.

6

And what, finally, of Roosevelt himself? It may seem too early to fix his position in our history, yet that position is reasonably clear. He takes his place in the great tradition of American liberalism, along with Jefferson, Jackson, Lincoln, Theodore Roosevelt and Wilson. Coming to office at a time when the very foundations of the republic seemed threatened and when men were beginning to despair of the ability of a constitutional democracy to meet a crisis, he restored confidence and proved that democracy could act as effectively in crisis as could totalitarian governments. A liberal, he put government clearly at the service of the people; a conservative, he pushed through reforms designed to strengthen the natural and human resources of the nation, restore agriculture and business to its former prosperity, and save capitalism. He saw that problems of government were primarily political, not economic; that politics should control economy — not economy, politics; and that politics was an art as well as a science. He repudiated isolationism, demanded for America once more her proper station and responsibility in world affairs, and, after unifying the American people on the major issues of aid to the democracies and war, furnished a war leadership bold, energetic and successful.

In all this Roosevelt was an opportunist — but an opportunist with a philosophy. He was the same kind of opportunist that Jefferson — that earlier "traitor to his class" — had been. The close view of Roosevelt has discovered numerous inconsistencies. But if we look back over Roosevelt's long career in politics — beginning with his fight on the Tammany machine in 1910 — we can see that amidst the hurly-burly of politics he has been unfalteringly consistent in his fundamental social and political philosophy. He has sought ends, and cheerfully adopted the "quarterback" technique with respect to means. And as the bitterness of particular controversies dies away, the larger outlines of his achievements during the past twelve years emerge with striking clarity. We can see that the promises of the New Deal platform of 1932 were carried out, more fully perhaps than those of any party platform since that of Polk a century ago. We can see that the promises of the inaugural address were fulfilled. We can see that the democratic philosophy which Roosevelt asserted was applied and implemented. Under his leadership the American people withstood the buffetings of depression and the fearful trial of war, and emerged strong and respected, refreshed in their faith in democracy and in the ultimate triumph of justice in human affairs.

"The only sure bulwark of continuing liberty," Roosevelt said, "is a government strong enough to protect the interests of the people, and a people strong enough and well enough informed to maintain its sovereign control over its government."

The Roosevelt administration proved once more that it was possible for such a government to exist and such a people to flourish, and restored to the United States its position as "the hope of the human race."

Walter Lippmann:

THE PERMANENT NEW DEAL

IT would be useful to know whether the many experiments of the past six years are merely a response to a passing emergency or whether they signify lasting changes in the relation between government and the economic order. A satisfactory answer to this question would not stop with a general conclusion that this is a rapidly changing world. The answer ought to carry conviction only if it identifies an important new function of government, defines it, and demonstrates the reason why there is a presumption of permanency. Burke has said that "one of the finest problems in legislation" is "to determine what the state ought to take upon itself to direct by the public wisdom, and what it ought to leave, with as little interference as possible, to individual exertion." Our inquiry is to find out, if we can, whether it has already been determined by historical circumstance that the state must henceforth direct certain affairs which hitherto have been left to private exertion.

It may be that we no longer have that perfect freedom of choice which Burke's remark implies, that a fundamental decision has already been made, and that our freedom to choose what ought to be the province of government is limited by that decision. Thus, for example, the question of American independence was a real one

before 1776; it was no longer an open question after the surrender of Cornwallis. The issue of a federal government as against a loose confederation was decided when Washington was inaugurated. The right of secession ceased to be real after Appomattox. President Wilson's plan of January, 1918, to create a federal state out of the old Austro-Hungarian empire passed into limbo when the subject nationalities revolted and declared their independence. After each of these decisive events the real issues were transformed. Must it be said that in an analogous sense we have recently passed decisively into a new relation between the government and the national economy?

Obviously, a contemporary opinion of this sort will be highly vulnerable. Not all the seedlings will become trees; to attempt to say which ones will flourish, which ones will wither away, is to enter a realm where certainty is impossible. Yet the living generation can hardly defer the attempt to understand its own actions because posterity will understand them better. Posterity will know — whereas we can only predict. It will see the consequences. We can only anticipate them. It will not be biased by our interests and our ignorance and our moods. We can only attempt to discount them. The disadvantages of foresight as compared with hindsight are insuperable. Yet somehow or other we have to find a method of analysis that will discount our bias and provide a reasonably objective criterion with which to distinguish the transitory from the permanent.

It has occurred to me that by a rather extraordinary accident there has been something like a controlled scientific demonstration. Perhaps we can take advantage of it in this inquiry. The Great Depression has run nearly six years. During the first half of this period Mr. Hoover and the Republicans were in power; during the second half, Mr. Roosevelt and the Democrats. They profess to be deeply opposed. Would it not be reasonable to assume that where we find a new principle and a new function of government common to both Mr. Hoover and Mr. Roosevelt, there is a strong presumption that we are in the presence of a change due to historical forces that transcend individuals and parties and their articulate programs? It is not proof. But proof is not to be had. It is merely a presumption. Is it not a strong presumption? Is there any other criterion available which is less likely to be the rationalization of our individual preferences? Is there any which more effectively discounts partisan bias? Or any which conforms more closely to ordinary experience? When men who think differently behave alike, is it not probable that they are both responding to forces that are stronger than their conscious beliefs?

Before we can begin to use this method of analysis we have to deal with the impression that the two Administrations are so radically different that they have nothing important in common. The partisans of both have tried to fix this opinion in the public mind. They would like us

to believe that a new era began on March 4, 1933. They would have us believe that Mr. Hoover was the faithful defender of the established traditions and that Mr. Roosevelt is the revolutionary pioneer of a New Deal. Though it will outrage the supporters of both men, I must argue that this is not history but partisan mythology: that though the two Presidents have somewhat different sympathies and allegiances, though they profess somewhat different purposes, though they have somewhat different constituencies to please, though they have resorted to somewhat different devices, yet in their fundamental conceptions of the functions of governments they are much nearer to each other than either is, let us say, to Calvin Coolidge or to Grover Cleveland.

I shall have to contend that if there has been anything in the nature of a sharp break with the past, the break occurred not in March, 1933, when Mr. Roosevelt was inaugurated but in the autumn of 1929 when, with the collapse of the post-war prosperity, President Hoover assumed the responsibility for recovery. No doubt, it was inevitable that he should have done this since he had been elected on the promise of four more years of prosperity. But that does not alter the fact that the policy initiated by President Hoover in the autumn of 1929 was something utterly unprecedented in American history. The national government undertook to make the whole economic order operate prosperously. In the language of Burke the state attempted to direct by the public wisdom a recovery in the business cycle which had hitherto been left with as little interference as possible to individual exertion. President Hoover, let us remember, did not merely seek to create an atmosphere of confidence in which private initiative could act; he intervened at every point in the national economy where he felt that something needed to be done.

For that reason, it may be said, I believe, that his historic position as a radical innovator has been greatly underestimated and that Mr. Roosevelt's pioneering has been greatly exaggerated. It was Mr. Hoover who abandoned the principles of *laissez faire* in relation to the business cycle, established the conviction that prosperity and depression can be publicly controlled by political action, and drove out of the public consciousness the old idea that depressions must be overcome by private adjustment.

Whether that was good or bad, necessary or unnecessary, does not concern us here. The point is that a radically new conception of the functions of government was established in the autumn of 1929. The subsequent course of events becomes utterly unintelligible if we accept naïvely what the partisans of Mr. Hoover and of Mr. Roosevelt say today. Only those who have forgotten the inclusive and persistent experimentation before March, 1933, can, I think, fail to see that most of President Roosevelt's recovery program is an evolution from President Hoover's program; and that there is a continuity of principle; and that both programs are derived from the unprecedented doctrine that the government is charged with responsibility for the successful operation of the economic order and the maintenance of a satisfactory standard of life for all classes in the nation. After October, 1929, that doctrine was the major premise of the Hoover Administration. It is the major premise of the Roosevelt Administration. Never, except in time of war, has it been the major premise in the policies of any other President. Did Harding in 1921 or Cleveland in 1893 or Grant in 1873 suppose that it was the President's duty to tell

farmers and business men and bankers, debtors and creditors, employers and employees, governors and mayors, what to do in order to restore prosperity, or that he had the right to draw upon all the powers of government and all the resources of the nation?

Yet that is precisely what President Hoover, beginning in the autumn of 1929, took to be his duty and his right. Not until his time had any American President assumed this specific responsibility with all the expansion of the functions of government which it necessarily implies. Yet when the change occurred, there was almost no comment. Almost no one raised his voice to challenge Mr. Hoover on the ground of the individualistic tradition or of the accepted limitations of the federal power. So we have a strong presumption that the great change was generated by historic circumstances that are stronger than the ordinary opinions of men.

2

On August 11, 1932, in accepting his renomination, President Hoover declared that when "the forces of destruction" invaded the American economy and brought about "bank and business failures, demoralization of security and real property values, commodity prices and employment, . . . two courses were open. We might have done nothing. That would have been utter ruin. Instead, we met the situation with proposals to private business and the Congress of the most gigantic program of economic defense and counter-attack ever evolved in the history of the republic."

Mr. Hoover made it perfectly plain that he had departed from the individualistic doctrine that depression must be liquidated by individual adjustment. "The function of the federal government in these times," he said, "is to *use its reserve powers* and its strength *for the protection of citizens and local governments* by support to our institutions *against forces beyond their control.*" He was insistent that this defensive and compensatory action by the government should not destroy but should on the contrary revive private and local enterprise and responsibility. But he had no doubts, theoretical or practical, indeed he proudly declared that "we have not feared boldly to adopt unprecedented measures to meet the unprecedented violence of the storm."

He then went on to describe his unprecedented measures. He had called the leaders of business and of labor and of agriculture "to meet with me and induced them, by their own initiative, to organize against panic:

"(1) To uphold wages until the cost of living was adjusted.

"(2) To spread existing employment through shortened hours.

"(3) To advance construction work, public and private, against future need."

He then described how he had mobilized the relief agencies and "when it became advisable to strengthen the States who could not longer carry the full burden of relief to distress, I held that the federal government should do so through loans to the States." He said that "in aid to unemployment we are expending some six hundred millions in federal construction and such public works as can be justified as bringing early and definite returns"; that in addition he had made "provision of one billion five hundred millions of loans to self-supporting works so that we may increase employment in productive labor."

He went on to tell how he had used government credit (1) to strengthen the capital of Federal Land Banks, (2) to lend money to farmers' cooperatives to protect farm prices and to homeowners

in danger of foreclosure, (3) to set up the Reconstruction Finance Corporation "with a capital of two billions to uphold the credit structure of the Nation."

He stated that "we expanded the functions and powers of the Federal Reserve Banks that they might counteract the stupendous shrinkage of credit due to fear, to hoarding and to foreign withdrawals."

He pointed out how, parallel with his expansion of the extraordinary expenditures of the government, he was seeking to retrench on the normal expenditures and to increase taxes to balance them.

Finally, he announced that "I am today organizing the private and financial resources of the country to coöperate effectively with the vast governmental instrumentalities which we have set in motion."

When Mr. Hoover declared that "these programs" were "unparalleled in the history of depressions in our country and in any time," he had perhaps overlooked a few other countries, but his claim was quite correct when confined to the United States. His program was unparalleled. But what interests us about it is that it lays down the fundamentally new principle that it is "the function of the federal government in these times to use its reserve powers and its strength" to regulate the business cycle, and that in applying this general principle Mr. Hoover formulated a program which contains all the more specific principles of Mr. Roosevelt's recovery program.

Let us fix in mind the working principles of Mr. Hoover's recovery program:

(1) To counteract deflation by a deliberate policy of inflating the base of credit.

(2) To draw upon the government credit in order to supplement the deficiency of private credit.

(3) To reduce the normal expenses of government but to incur extraordinary expenditures covered not by taxation but by deficit financing.

(4) To expand public works in order to create employment.

(5) To have the federal government assume the ultimate responsibility for relief of destitution where local or private resources are inadequate.

(6) To reduce the hours of labor while maintaining wage rates.

(7) To peg farm prices and encourage farmers to organize to curtail production.

(8) To organize industry with a view to adopting common policies in respect to wages, hours, prices, and capital investment.

Apart from the Roosevelt measures of reform, which we shall have to examine later, all the main features of the Roosevelt program were anticipated by Mr. Hoover.

3

The only important difference between the monetary policies of the two Administrations is that Mr. Hoover attempted to regulate the internal value of the dollar whereas Mr. Roosevelt is attempting to regulate its external value as well. Mr. Hoover was just as eager as Mr. Roosevelt has been to bring about a rise in the wholesale prices of staple commodities, particularly the politically sensitive farm products and raw materials whose prices are fixed by international competition. He was just as eager to stop the general deflation and to bring about a reflation. Nor did he hesitate to use monetary measures, sometimes called "currency tinkering."

The measures he used consisted in expanding the base of credit by open-market operations in the Federal Reserve system and in lowering the discount rates. This was the policy of the President, of the Treasury, and of his appointees on the Federal Reserve Board It was carried out in spite of some opposition from some of the Federal Reserve

Banks, and though the government's right to regulate the volume of credit was not formally avowed, as it is in Governor Eccles's banking bill, the power was, in fact, exercised.

Mr. Roosevelt has continued this policy. He has supplemented it by measures designed to regulate the international value of the dollar in terms of gold, silver, and the foreign exchanges. But the major premise, which was that the regulation of the purchasing power of money is a function of government and is not automatic, was accepted and acted upon by the Hoover Administration. However great may be the differences of opinion as to how the purchasing power of money should be regulated, however much men may disagree as to who shall exercise the power to regulate, it would therefore seem reasonable to assume that the effort to manage the purchasing power of money will continue to be a function of government.

Legally it has, of course, always been a function of government, and ever since the war we have had a managed monetary system. Neither Mr. Hoover nor Mr. Roosevelt invented a managed currency. Yet they have changed the conception of what the object of management should be. It had previously been assumed, though not with entire consistency, that the dominant purpose of management should be to keep the currency stable in terms of gold. Mr. Hoover did that though he wished at the same time to regulate the currency in terms of its purchasing power. When the value of gold changed violently between 1929 and 1933, he was caught on the horns of a dilemma. If he regulated the currency to maintain a stable gold content he had a currency which was catastrophically unstable in its purchasing power. Mr.

Roosevelt resolved the difficulty in 1933 by abandoning stability in terms of gold in order to achieve control in terms of purchasing power. But in 1934 he returned to stability in terms of gold, and ever since the American price level has once more been under the disturbing influence of the instability of gold itself. The effort to manage the value of gold by manipulating the value of silver followed. It is too early to judge the experiment when this is written. Whether it fails or succeeds, whether the outcome is a new international gold standard, or bimetallism, or a second abandonment of the gold standard, is outside this discussion. The idea that it is a function of public authority to regulate the purchasing power of money is not likely to be abandoned, whatever may be the fate of the particular measures now used to regulate it.

The use of the national credit to support and to supplement local and private credit is not, strictly speaking, a radically new innovation. It was practiced during the World War and in the first post-war depression. President Hoover adopted the policy on a grand scale when he created the Reconstruction Finance Corporation and various farm credit agencies. Mr. Roosevelt has continued the policy and has extended it. A substantial part of the deficits incurred in both Administrations is due not to the expenses of government but to this banking operation. Neither President has believed that the money borrowed by the government for this banking operation should be balanced by taxes. Both have acted on the principle that this banking operation should be supported by deficit financing. It is reasonable to suppose that this principle will become orthodox and that in future emergencies government borrowing will be resorted to when private credit is deficient.

The questionable element of the Roosevelt budgetary program is in that part of the deficit which is being deliberately incurred in irrecoverable expenditures — for relief and for public works that are not "self-liquidating." Mr. Hoover had deficits of this sort. But he had a bad conscience about them, whereas Mr. Roosevelt has seemed to look upon them as preferable in princi ple to the deflationary effect of greatly increased taxes or of drastic retrenchment. But while Mr. Hoover was not in favor of deficits to finance public works, he was, of course, an early and conspicuous promoter of the idea that government enterprises should be expanded when private enterprises contract. He formulated the principle during the depression of 1921, acted upon it in 1930, and pointed to it with pride in 1932. Mr. Hoover believed in the principle of "pump-priming." In actual fact, he financed his pump-priming with deficits just as Mr. Roosevelt has done. In theory, he would presumably have preferred to finance them by taxes in order to keep the budget in balance, and presumably he would today prefer to give up the pump-priming in order to balance the budget.

In their relations to agriculture and to industry there is no sharp break between the two Administrations. Both have recognized that the agricultural staples have unsheltered prices whereas most manu factured goods have sheltered prices, and that this produces a disparity which it is a function of government to correct. The superior position of industry lies in the fact that it can benefit by the tariff, that much of it is under a centralized control in which prices can be maintained by regulating the supply through curtailment of production. The agricultural staples, on the other hand, cannot without special devices take advantage of tariffs, and the farmers are the most highly individualistic and competitive of all producers. President Hoover made many attempts to remedy this disparity. He increased the tariff on farm products. He used government money in an effort to control the supply offered in the markets. He advised the farmers to curtail production, and he contemplated the government rental or purchase of marginal lands in order permanently to reduce production. The Roosevelt agricultural policy has followed those same principles. It has used government money to regulate the supply offered for sale. It has supplemented Mr. Hoover's advice to curtail production by levying a tax to pay farmers who follow the advice, and it is withdrawing marginal lands permanently. Both Presidents recognized that a satisfactory domestic solution of the farm problem is very unlikely; both have wanted to see a revival of foreign markets; neither was able or willing to expand agricultural exports by reducing the tariff on industrial goods.

As regards their relations to industry, if we strip the N.R.A. of its ballyhoo, of the more or less unenforceable and unenforced labor provisions, we find the trade associations (which Mr. Hoover did so much to promote as Secretary of Commerce) freed of the menace of the anti-trust laws (which Mr. Hoover as President did so little to enforce). The N.R.A. extended the principle of organization to industries and trades that had not been organized previously. It tightened up the organization all along the line. It made price-fixing and production control and marketing quotas more general, more effective, more respectable.

But in embryo, in all its essential features, the substance of N.R.A. existed before the Blue Eagle was hatched. The National Industry Recovery Act was little more than the substitution of legal for companionate marriages in the realm of private monopoly.

Even the wage policy of N.R.A. was a continuation of a policy inaugurated by Mr. Hoover in the autumn of 1929 and maintained by him throughout his term. It consisted in the preservation of the rate of wages regardless of the income received by the wage-earner. Mr. Hoover threw the whole weight of his influence against reduction in the rate of wages, as Mr. Roosevelt did in 1933 and until very recent times. He believed what the labor leaders believed, what the N.R.A. economists believed, what Mr. Roosevelt in his first year believed, that the purchasing power of labor could be maintained by a high hourly rate. That the high hourly rate in the face of falling prices was a sure way to increase and perpetuate unemployment was denied in both Administrations, though I suspect that neither Mr. Hoover nor Mr. Roosevelt would deny it today.

In rough fashion, this covers the ground usually marked out as the recovery program. I do not see how one can fail to conclude that in all essential matters of policy – dealing with monetary management, the budget, the agricultural disparity, and industrial "stabilization" – there has been no break in principle, and that the Roosevelt measures are a continuous evolution of the Hoover measures.

What about the reforms? In one sense the most radical of all the reforms are these very recovery measures themselves: the acceptance by the government of responsibility for recovery, and the corollaries of that – the resort to monetary management, the use of government credit, the expansion of government enterprise, and the organization of agriculture and of industry under government auspices for the control of production and of supply in the markets. These mark great changes in a political system which until 1929 was committed to the general doctrine of *laissez faire.*

The measures which are specifically called the "reforms" are distinguished from the others by the fact that, except as a response to the challenge of popular discontent, they were not dictated by the emergency and might have been imposed later and in more leisurely fashion. But it is clear, I think, that though the reforms might have been delayed, and though they might have been different in detail, their essential principles are derived directly and inevitably from the fundamental assumption of the whole period since 1929, that we have a national economy and not a mere aggregation of individual enterprises.

The reforms extend into new fields the regulation of private enterprises on the one hand, and the expansion of government enterprises on the other. Some of the new regulation is merely the logical development of well-established principles. The clearest example in this category is the legislation as to busses and trucks and other common carriers in order to bring about parity of competitive conditions with the railroads. Another example in the same category is the proposal to bring gas and electricity under more complete regulation. These reforms involve no new principles, and the fundamental questions they raise are not novel and are not radical.

In the present Administration we come soon, however, to regulations which are novel and radical. In the Securities Act and in the Stock Exchange Act and in certain parts of the Banking Act of 1933, the orbit of public authority is enlarged. In substance, these reforms lay down the principle that corporations financed by public subscription are publicly accountable. They require a disclosure, particularly of the whole process of capital investment, which is intended to take from private management much of its former privacy. The underlying theory of the legislation is that when the ownership of corporations is widely diffused, when corporations are financed out of the savings of large masses of people, it is an anomaly that those who control and manage them but do not own them should have the kind of privacy in their corporate conduct which men have in their genuinely personal affairs and in the handling of truly personal property. The legislation in these three acts is not socialism. It does not substitute government ownership or government management for private ownership and management. It lays down the rule that private management shall operate in the public view in order to make it accountable to the great mass of its owners, its creditors, its customers, and its employees.

The officers of corporations are in effect required to submit to the same standards which they would have to meet if they were public officials. The doctrine that public office is a public trust is supplemented by the doctrine that corporate office is a public trust. From this doctrine there follow inevitably the prohibitions in the new laws against being on both sides of a transaction. Just as a public official may not have a private interest in a contract with the government, so under the new laws bankers may not sell to their depositors securities which they have issued; utility holding companies may not sell services at their own price to operating companies they control; it is made hard for the officers and directors of corporations to use their special knowledge for their private advantage, and they are required to disclose their private interests in the corporations they manage.

That this development of public policy is the logical consequence of the corporate form of industry seems plain. It might have come more slowly had the public not suffered such losses after 1929, and if there had not been so many flagrant examples of the abuse of positions of trust. But once so important a part of the property of the nation became organized in large corporations, it was only a question of when and of how they would be recognized as being public institutions in all their essential relations.

The transition to this new conception of policy might possibly have been delayed a few years had the accidents of politics brought a conservative rather than a progressive administration into power in 1933. The impulses of reform generated in the upheaval of the nineties were held back for a few years by the reaction against Bryanism and the distraction of the Spanish War. They became effective about 1902 and were not exhausted until the World War introduced a new diversion of the national energy. The reforms of Theodore Roosevelt and of Woodrow Wilson brought under some regulation large areas of private enterprise: the railroads, the central banking function, the public domain and natural resources, foods and drugs. These present reforms extend to private finance, generally, and to the capital market, the underlying assumptions which were applied to railroads and central banking in the preceding era of reforms.

In addition to this extension of the regulatory functions of government, there has been an extension of government enterprise. A part of it is simply a development of the conservation movement. Reforestation, measures against soil erosion, the protection of watercourses are not new in principle: it has long been recognized that there were certain kinds of capital investment which, because they could not be profitable to private enterprise, had to be undertaken collectively. Mr. Roosevelt has, however, made a departure in at least two important directions. The first is represented by the Tennessee Valley Authority: here collective enterprise has been deliberately undertaken for the purpose of making a competitive demonstration against the electric utility companies. The second is the social insurance program: here the federal government enters a field heretofore left to individual or local action.

It would be an exaggeration to say that either of these Roosevelt reforms represents a clean break with the past. No other President, it is true, ever sought to regulate electric utilities by forcing them to face the competition of government-owned utilities. But other Presidents have sought to regulate railroad rates by building canals, and President Hoover himself promoted the St. Lawrence Seaway as a competitor with the railroads. As for social insurance, while it represents a new function of the federal government, it is not a new function in state government, and Republican leaders, including Mr. Hoover, have endorsed it in principle.

We must conclude, I think, that however startling they may have seemed, however inadvisable or inexpedient it may have been to impose them at this time, the Roosevelt reforms are far less novel or radical in their implications than is the recovery program which Mr. Hoover and Mr. Roosevelt have both followed. To regulate large corporations and high finance, to extend government enterprise into fields unoccupied by private enterprise, to use government enterprise as a threat to compel private monopoly to reduce its rates, to insure the weaker members of the community by collective action — none of these things is new in principle. They are all the continuation of a movement in American politics which goes back at least fifty years, and there is little if anything in the New Deal reforms which was not implicit in the New Nationalism of Theodore Roosevelt or the New Freedom of Woodrow Wilson.

The recovery program, on the other hand, is new and is radical. For here we have an assumption of responsibility for the operation of the whole national economy and the conviction that all the reserve power of government and all the resources it can command may and must be used to defend the standard of life of the people "against forces beyond their control."

This represents a far more radical change in the conception of government in America than is to be found in any of the reforms. For if it is now the responsibility of the government to protect the people against the consequences of depression, then inevitably the government must regulate the prosperity which precedes depression and produces it. If government is responsible for the downward phase of the business cycle, it has a responsibility in the whole business cycle. If it is fitting and necessary to manage the currency, the national credit, budgetary expenditures, and the like to counteract deflation, then it is fitting and necessary that they be managed to counteract inflation.

It would seem that the decision which Mr. Hoover took in the autumn of 1929 is irreversible: he committed the government to the new function of using all its powers to regulate the business cycle. With this precedent established it is almost inconceivable that any of his successors should in another depression refuse to act. The knowledge that the government will have to act to offset depression compels it to act to prevent depression. Because Mr. Hoover and Mr. Roosevelt have regulated a slump, their successors will also have to regulate a boom. The business cycle has been placed within the orbit of government, and for *laissez faire* and individual adjustment and liquidation there has been substituted conscious management by the political state.

It is perhaps possible to go further and indicate why it is that this very great new duty has been imposed upon the state. The recovery program since 1929 has rested on the basic assumption that the "fixed costs" in a modern economy are rigid: that debts, contracts, wage rates, taxes cannot be reduced quickly or easily or sufficiently to liquidate the depression. Part of the recovery program under both Mr. Hoover and Mr. Roosevelt has in fact been a defense of rigid wage rates and debts. The classic remedy, the only remedy known to *laissez faire*, is therefore impracticable. But if "fixed costs" are rigid, then flexibility must develop somewhere else in the economy if there is not to be complete paralysis followed by a social collapse. The flexibility to compensate for the rigidity of "fixed costs" has been found in the currency, in the national budget, and in public expenditure.

Unless one is to suppose that the proportion of fixed debt in the modern economy will be drastically reduced, that long-term contracts and rentals will become easily amended, that salaries, wages, and pensions will become easily adjustable, we may take it as certain that we shall not return to *laissez faire* in the business cycle. If we do not return to it, then the management of money and the use of the national credit to expand and to contract government expenditures must be regarded as permanent functions of the American government.

No one will imagine that I am saying that the particular devices employed by Mr. Hoover or Mr. Roosevelt were well conceived or effectively administered. To judge them, we should have to examine them on their merits. But I am saying that when we examine them, we are compelled to judge them on the presumption that, because our economy has become too rigid to readjust itself by individual action, it will henceforth be a normal function of government to attempt to regulate the business cycle. We have come on to a new plateau from which it is not likely that we shall easily descend. On this plateau the issues of the near future will be fought out, and there it will be determined whether a system of private enterprise, which has lost much of its power to adjust itself, can be preserved in working equilibrium by the compensatory action of the state.

Franklin D. Roosevelt: THREE ADDRESSES

1. CAMPAIGN ADDRESS, DETROIT, MICHIGAN, OCTOBER 2, 1932

MY OLD FRIEND MAYOR MURPHY, MY OLD FRIEND GOVERNOR COMSTOCK, AND YOU — MANY OF YOU — MY OLD FRIENDS OF DETROIT AND OF MICHIGAN:

YOU know today is Sunday, and I am afraid that some of you people today in Detroit have been talking politics. Well, I am not going to. I want to talk to you about Government. That is a very different thing. And I am not going to refer to parties at all.

I am going to refer to some of the fundamentals that antedate parties, and antedate republics and empires, fundamentals that are as old as mankind itself. They are fundamentals that have been expressed in philosophies, for I don't know how many thousands of years, in every part of the world. Today, in our boasted modern civilization, we are facing just exactly the same problem, just exactly the same conflict between two schools of philosophy that they faced in the earliest days of America, and indeed of the world. One of them — one of these old philosophies — is the philosophy of those who would "let things alone." The other is the philosophy that strives for something new — something that the human race has never attained yet, but something which I believe the human race can and will attain — social justice, through social action.

From the days of the cave man to the days of the automobile, the philosophy of "letting things alone" has resulted in the jungle law of the survival of the so-called fittest. The philosophy of social action results in the protection of humanity and the fitting of as many human beings as possible into the scheme of surviving. I am sorry to say that among the followers of that first philosophy of "letting things alone" are a lot of people in my community back home, which is a little village, and in the farming districts of the Nation and in the great cities, such as yours. We can place in that philosophy a great many splendid people who keep saying, not only to themselves and to their friends, but to the community as a whole, "Why shouldn't we 'let things alone'? In the first place they are not as bad as they are painted, and in the second place they will cure themselves. Time is a great healer." An easy philosophy! The kind of philosophy, my friends, that was expressed the other day by a Cabinet officer of the United States of America, when he is reported to have said, "Our children are apt to profit rather than suffer from what is going on."

While he was saying that, another branch of our Government, the United States Public Health Service, which believes in my kind of philosophy, I think, said this: "Over six millions of our pub-

From *The Public Papers and Addresses of Franklin D. Roosevelt*, ed. Samuel I. Rosenman (Vols. I–V, Random House, 1938; Vols. VI–IX, Macmillan, 1941), I, 771–780; V, 383–390; VI, 113–121. Reprinted by permission of the editor.

lic school children do not have enough to eat. Many of them are fainting at their desks. They are a prey to disease. Their future health is menaced."

In which school do you believe?

In the same way, there are two theories of prosperity and of well-being: The first theory is that if we make the rich richer, somehow they will let a part of their prosperity trickle down to the rest of us. The second theory — and I suppose this goes back to the days of Noah — I won't say Adam and Eve, because they had a less complicated situation — but, at least, back in the days of the flood, there was the theory that if we make the average of mankind comfortable and secure, their prosperity will rise upward, just as yeast rises up, through the ranks.

Now, my friends, the philosophy of social justice that I am going to talk about this Sabbath day, the philosophy of social justice through social action, calls definitely, plainly, for the reduction of poverty. And what do we mean when we talk about the reduction of poverty? We mean the reduction of the causes of poverty. When we have an epidemic of disease in these modern days, what do we do? We turn in the first instance to find out the sources from which the disease has come; and when we have found those sources, those causes, we turn the energy of our attack upon them.

We have got beyond the point in modern civilization of merely trying to fight an epidemic of disease by taking care of the victims after they are stricken. We do that; but we do more. We seek to prevent it; and the attack on poverty is not very unlike the attack on disease. We are seeking the causes and when we have found them, we must turn our attack upon them. What are the causes that destroy human beings, driving millions of them to destruction? Well, there

are a good many of them, and there are a good many of us who are alive today who have seen tremendous steps taken toward the eradication of those causes.

Take, for instance, ill health: You and I know what has been accomplished by community effort, State effort, and the efforts and association of individual men and women toward the bettering of the health of humanity.

We have spent vast sums upon research. We have established a wholly new science, the science of public health; and we are carrying what we call today "instruction in health" into the most remote corners of our cities and our country districts. Apart from the humanitarian aspect, the result has been an economic saving. It has been money which has been returned to the community a thousand times over. You and I know that a sick person — a man, woman or child, who has to be taken care of — not only takes the individual who is sick out of active participation and useful citizenship, but takes somebody else, too. And so, from the purely dollars and cents point of view that we Americans are so fond of thinking about, public health has paid for itself.

And what have we done along other lines for the prevention of some of the causes of poverty?

I go back twenty-two years to a time when, in my State of New York, we tried to pass in the Legislature what we called a Workmen's Compensation Act, knowing, as we did, that there were thousands of men and women who every year were seriously injured in industrial accidents of one kind or another, who became a burden on their community, who were unable to work, unable to get adequate medical care. A lot of us youngsters in the Legislature in those days were called radicals. We were called Socialists. They did not know the word Bolshevik in those days, but if they had known that, we would have been called that, too. We put through a Workmen's Compensation Act. The courts, thinking in terms of the Seventeenth Century, as some courts do, declared it to be unconstitutional. So we had to go about amending the Constitution, and the following year we got a Workmen's Compensation Act.

What has it done? We were not the first State to have it. One of the earliest States, by the way, was New Jersey, which, the year before the action in the State of New York, passed a Workmen's Compensation Act at the bidding of that great humanitarian Governor, Woodrow Wilson. The result has been that almost every State of the Union has eliminated that cause of poverty among the masses of the people.

Take another form of poverty in the old days. Not so long ago, there were in every part of the Nation — in country districts and in city districts — hundreds and thousands of crippled children who could get no adequate care, who were lost to the community and who were a burden on the community. We have, in these past twenty or thirty years, gradually provided means for restoring crippled children to useful citizenship; and it has all been a factor in going after and solving one of the causes of poverty and disease.

And then in these later years, we have been wondering about old people; and we have come to the conclusion in this modern civilization that the old-fashioned theory of carting old people off to the county poorhouse is not the best thing after all.

I shall tell you what sold me on old age insurance — old age pensions. Not so long ago — about ten years — I received a great shock. I had been away from my home town of Hyde Park during the winter time and when I came back I found that a tragedy had occurred. I had had an old farm neighbor, who had been a splendid old fellow — Supervisor of his town, Highway Commissioner of his town, one of the best of our citizens. Before I had left, around Christmas time, I had seen the old man, who was eighty-nine, his old brother, who was eighty-seven, his other brother, who was eighty-five, and his "kid" sister, who was eighty-three.

They were living on a farm; I knew it was mortgaged to the hilt; but I assumed that everything was all right, for they still had a couple of cows and a few chickens. But when I came back in the spring, I found that in the severe winter that followed there had been a heavy fall of snow, and one of the old brothers had fallen down on his way out to the barn to milk the cow, and had perished in the snow drift. The town authorities had come along and had taken the two old men and had put them into the county poorhouse, and they had taken the old lady and had sent her down, for want of a better place, to the insane asylum, although she was not insane but just old.

That sold me on the idea of trying to keep homes intact for old people.

In another respect modern science has been good to us. It is not so very long ago that a young person, or an old person, who had any trouble with his mentality, was put into what was called an asylum and not long before that they used to call it a "madhouse." Even when I was a boy, the States of the Nation used to provide asylums. And when anybody was not entirely right mentally — when anyone was a mental defective as we would say today — he used to be carted off to the asylum to stay there until he came out to go to the graveyard.

Today that is no longer true. Medical science is now doing two things: first, for the young people who are not mentally deficient but who require special mental training we are applying special treatment and special education so that, instead of becoming a burden when they grow up, they are going to be useful citizens.

And then, on the other side of it, there is the special treatment for the older people, who do have to go to hospitals for mental troubles. The other day, just before I left Albany, I got a report from my State Department of Mental Hygiene showing that instead of the old-fashioned system in which the rule was observed of "once in, always in," this past year in the State of New York we had sent back to their families 23 percent of all those who were in our hospitals for mental cases — cured.

Now, those are some of the causes that have destroyed in past ages countless thousands of our fellow human beings. They are the causes that we must attack if we are to make the future safer for humanity. We can go on taking care of the handicapped and the crippled and the sick and the feeble-minded and the unemployed; but common sense and humanity call on us to turn our back definitely on these destroyers. Poverty resulting from these destroyers is largely preventable, but, my friends, if poverty is to be prevented, we require a broad program of social justice.

We cannot go back to the old prisons, for example, to the old system of mere punishment under which a man out of prison was not fitted to live in our community alongside of us. We cannot go back to the old system of asylums. We cannot go back to the old lack of hospitals, the lack of public health. We cannot

go back to the sweatshops of America. We cannot go back to children working in factories. Those days are gone.

There are a lot of new steps to take. It is not a question of just not going back. It is a question also of not standing still.

For instance, the problem of unemployment in the long run — and I am not talking about the emergency of this year — can be and shall be solved by the human race. Some leaders have wisely declared for a system of unemployment insurance throughout this broad land of ours; and we are going to come to it.

But I do not believe the Secretary of the Interior would be for it. He would say that great good is coming to this country because of the present situation. Yes, the followers of the philosophy of "let alone" have been decrying all of these measures of social welfare. What do they call them? They call them "paternalistic." All right, if they are paternalistic, I am a father.

They maintain that these laws interfere with individualism, forgetful of the fact that the causes of poverty in the main are beyond the control of any one individual or any czar, either a czar of politics or a czar of industry. The followers of the philosophy of "social action for the prevention of poverty" maintain that if we set up a system of justice we shall have small need for the exercise of mere philanthropy. Justice, after all, is the first goal we seek. We believe that when justice has been done individualism will have a greater security to devote the best that individualism itself can give. In other words, my friends, our long-range objective is not a dole, but a job.

At the same time, we have throughout this Nation — and I know you have in Detroit, because Frank Murphy has talked to me of it many times in the past year or two — widespread suffering which all of us in the city and country alike have to do everything we can to tide over. All agree that the first responsibility for the alleviation of poverty and distress and for the care of the victims of the depression rests upon the locality — its individuals, organizations and Government. It rests, first of all, perhaps, upon the private agencies of philanthropy, secondly, other social organizations, and last, but not least, the Church. Yet all agree that to leave to the locality the entire responsibility would result in placing the heaviest burden in most cases upon those who are the least able to bear it. In other words, the communities that have the most difficult problem, like Detroit, would be the communities that would have to bear the heaviest of the burdens.

And so the State should step in to equalize the burden by providing for a large portion of the care of the victims of poverty and by providing assistance and guidance for local communities.

Above and beyond that duty of the States the national Government has a responsibility.

I would like to enlarge on that a lot, but that would be politics, and I cannot. My friends, the ideal of social justice of which I have spoken — an ideal that years ago might have been thought overadvanced — is now accepted by the moral leadership of all of the great religious groups of the country. Radical? Yes, and I shall show you how radical it is. I am going to cite three examples of what the churches say, the radical churches of America — Protestant, Catholic and Jewish.

And first I will read to you from the Sunday Sermon, the Labor Sermon sent out this year by the Federal Council of Churches of Christ in America, representing a very large proportion of the Protestants in our country.

Hear how radical they are: They say:

The thing that matters in any industrial system is what it does actually to human beings. . . .

It is not denied that many persons of wealth are rendering great service to society. It is only suggested that the wealthy are overpaid in sharp contrast with the underpaid masses of the people. The concentration of wealth carries with it a dangerous concentration of power. It leads to conflict and violence. To suppress the symptoms of this inherent conflict while leaving the fundamental causes of it untouched is neither sound statesmanship nor Christian goodwill.

It is becoming more and more clear that the principles of our religion and the findings of social sciences point in the same direction. Economists now call attention to the fact that the present distribution of wealth and income, which is so unbrotherly in the light of Christian ethics, is also unscientific in that it does not furnish purchasing power to the masses to balance consumption and production in our machine age.

And now I am going to read you another great declaration and I wonder how many people will call it radical. It is just as radical as I am. It is a declaration from one of the greatest forces of conservatism in the world, the Catholic Church. I quote, my friends, from the scholarly encyclical issued last year by the Pope, one of the greatest documents of modern times:

It is patent in our days that not alone is wealth accumulated, but immense power and despotic economic domination are concentrated in the hands of a few, and that those few are frequently not the owners but only the trustees and directors of invested funds which they administer at their good pleasure. . . .

This accumulation of power, the characteristic note of the modern economic order, is a natural result of limitless free competition, which permits the survival of those only who are the strongest, which often means those who fight most relentlessly, who pay least heed to the dictates of conscience.

This concentration of power has led to a three-fold struggle for domination: First, there is the struggle for dictatorship in the economic sphere itself; then the fierce battle to acquire control of the Government, so that its resources and authority may be abused in the economic struggle, and, finally, the clash between the Governments themselves.

And finally, I would read to you from another great statement, a statement from Rabbi Edward L. Israel, Chairman of the Social Justice Commission of the Central Conference of American Rabbis. Here is what he says:

We talk of the stabilization of business. What we need is the stabilization of human justice and happiness and the permanent employment of economic policies which will enable us to preserve the essential human values of life amid all the changing aspects of the economic order. We must have a revamping of the entire method of approach to these problems of the economic order. We need a new type of social conscience that will give us courage to act. . . .

We so easily forget. Once the cry of so-called prosperity is heard in the land, we all become so stampeded by the spirit of the god Mammon, that we cannot serve the dictates of social conscience. . .   We are here to serve notice that the economic order is the invention of man; and that it cannot dominate certain eternal principles of justice and of God.

And so, my friends, I feel a little as if I had been preaching a sermon. I feel a little as if I had been talking too much of some of the fundamentals, and yet those fundamentals enter into your life and my life every day. More, perhaps, than we can realize. If we realized that far more, it would result throughout this country in a greater activity, a greater interest on the part of the individual men and women who make up our Nation, in some of the problems which cannot be solved in the long run without the help of everybody.

We need leadership, of course. We need leadership of people who are honest in their thinking and honest in their doing. We need leadership if it is straight thinking and unselfish; but in the last analysis we must have the help of the men and women all the way from the top to the bottom, especially of the men and women who believe in the school of philosophy which is not content to leave things as they are.

And so, in these days of difficulty, we Americans everywhere must and shall choose the path of social justice — the only path that will lead us to a permanent bettering of our civilization, the path that our children must tread and their children must tread, the path of faith, the path of hope and the path of love toward our fellow man.

2. ADDRESS AT THE DEMOCRATIC STATE CONVENTION
SYRACUSE, NEW YORK, SEPTEMBER 29, 1936

LADIES AND GENTLEMEN:

FROM force of long habit I almost said, "My fellow delegates."

Tonight you and I join forces for the 1936 campaign. We enter it with confidence. Never was there greater need for fidelity to the underlying conception of Americanism than there is today. And once again it is given to our party to carry the message of that Americanism to the people.

The task on our part is twofold: First, as simple patriotism requires, to separate the false from the real issues; and, secondly, with facts and without rancor, to clarify the real problems for the American public.

There will be — there are — many false issues. In that respect, this will be no different from other campaigns. Partisans, not willing to face realities, will drag out red herrings — as they have always done — to divert attention from the trail of their own weaknesses.

This practice is as old as our democracy. Avoiding the facts — fearful of the truth — a malicious opposition charged that George Washington planned to make himself king under a British form of government; that Thomas Jefferson planned to set up a guillotine under a French Revolutionary form of government; that Andrew Jackson soaked the rich of the Eastern seaboard and planned to surrender American democracy to the dictatorship of a frontier mob. They called Abraham Lincoln a Roman Emperor; Theodore Roosevelt a Destroyer; Woodrow Wilson a self-constituted Messiah.

In this campaign another herring turns up. In former years it has been British and French — and a variety of other things. This year it is Russian. Desperate in mood, angry at failure, cunning in purpose, individuals and groups are seeking to make Communism an issue in an election where Communism is not a controversy between the two major parties.

Here and now, once and for all, let us bury that red herring, and destroy that false issue. You are familiar with my background; you know my heritage; and you are familiar, especially in the State of New York, with my public service extending back over a quarter of a century. For nearly four years I have been President of the United States. A long record has been written. In that record, both in this State and in the national capital, you will find a simple, clear and consistent adherence not only to the letter, but to the spirit of the American form of government.

To that record, my future and the future of my Administration will conform. I have not sought, I do not seek, I repudiate the support of any advocate of Communism or of any other alien "ism" which would by fair means or foul change our American democracy.

That is my position. It always has been my position. It always will be my position.

There is no difference between the major parties as to what they think about Communism. But there is a very great difference between the two parties in what they do about Communism.

I must tell you why. Communism is a manifestation of the social unrest which always comes with widespread economic maladjustment. We in the Democratic party have not been content merely to denounce this menace. We have been realistic enough to face it. We have been intelligent enough to do something about it. And the world has seen the results of what we have done.

In the spring of 1933 we faced a crisis which was the ugly fruit of twelve years of neglect of the causes of economic and social unrest. It was a crisis made to order for all those who would overthrow our form of government. Do I need to recall to you the fear of those days — the reports of those who piled supplies in their basements, who laid plans to get their fortunes across the border, who got themselves hideaways in the country against the impending upheaval? Do I need to recall the law-abiding heads of peaceful families, who began to wonder, as they saw their children starve, how they would get the bread they saw in the bakery window? Do I need to recall the homeless boys who were traveling in bands through the countryside seeking work, seeking food — desperate because they could find neither? Do I need to recall the farmers who banded together with pitchforks to keep the sheriff from selling the farm home under foreclosure? Do I need to recall the powerful leaders of industry and banking who came to me in Washington in those early days of 1933 pleading to be saved?

Most people in the United States remember today the fact that starvation was averted, that homes and farms were saved, that banks were reopened, that crop prices rose, that industry revived, and that the dangerous forces subversive of our form of government were turned aside.

A few people — a few only — unwilling to remember, seem to have forgotten those days.

In the summer of 1933, a nice old gentleman wearing a silk hat fell off the end of a pier. He was unable to swim. A friend ran down the pier, dived overboard and pulled him out; but the silk hat floated off with the tide. After the old gentleman had been revived, he was effusive in his thanks. He praised his friend for saving his life. Today, three years later, the old gentleman is berating his friend because the silk hat was lost.

Why did that crisis of 1929 to 1933 pass without disaster?

The answer is found in the record of what we did. Early in the campaign of 1932 I said: "To meet by reaction that danger of radicalism is to invite disaster. Reaction is no barrier to the radical, it is a challenge, a provocation. The way to meet that danger is to offer a workable program of reconstruction, and the party to offer it is the party with clean hands." We met the emergency with emergency action. But far more important than that, we went to the roots of the problem, and attacked the cause of the crisis. We were against revolution. Therefore, we waged war against those conditions which make revolutions — against the inequalities and resentments which breed them. In America in 1933 the people did not attempt to remedy wrongs by overthrowing their institutions. Americans were made to realize that wrongs could and would be set right within their institutions. We proved that democracy can work.

I have said to you that there is a very great difference between the two parties in what they do about Communism. Conditions congenial to Communism were being bred and fostered throughout this Nation up to the very day of March 4, 1933. Hunger was breeding it, loss of homes and farms was breeding it, closing banks were breeding it, a ruinous price level was breeding it. Discontent and fear were spreading through the land. The previous national Administration, bewildered, did nothing.

In their speeches they deplored it, but by their actions they encouraged it. The injustices, the inequalities, the downright suffering out of which revolutions come — what did they do about these things? Lacking courage, they evaded. Being selfish, they neglected. Being short-sighted, they ignored. When the crisis came — as these wrongs made it sure to come — America was unprepared.

Our lack of preparation for it was best proved by the cringing and the fear of the very people whose indifference helped to make the crisis. They came to us pleading that we should do, over-night, what they should have been doing through the years.

And the simple causes of our unpreparedness were two: First, a weak leadership, and, secondly, an inability to see causes, to understand the reasons for social unrest — the tragic plight of 90 per cent of the men, women and children who made up the population of the United States.

It has been well said that "The most dreadful failure of which any form of government can be guilty is simply to lose touch with reality, because out of this failure all imaginable forms of evil grow. Every empire that has crashed has come down primarily because its rulers did not know what was going on in the world and were incapable of learning."

It is for that reason that our American form of government will continue to be safest in Democratic hands. The real, actual, undercover Republican leadership is the same as it was four years ago. That leadership will never comprehend the need for a program of social justice and of regard for the well-being of the masses of our people.

I have been comparing leadership in Washington. This contrast between Democratic and Republican leadership holds true throughout the length and breadth of the State of New York. As far back as the year 1910, the old Black Horse Cavalry in Albany, which we old people will remember, was failing to meet changing social conditions by appropriate social legislation. Here was a State noted for its industry and noted for its agriculture — a State with the greatest mixture of population — where the poorest and the richest lived, literally, within a stone's throw of each other — in short a situation made to order for potential unrest. And yet in this situation the best that the Republican leaders of those days could say was: "Let them eat cake." What would have happened if that reactionary domination had continued through all these hard years?

Starting in 1911, a Democratic leadership came into power, and with it a new philosophy of government. I had the good fortune to come into public office at that time. I found other young men in the Legislature — men who held the same philosophy; one of them was Bob Wagner; another was Al Smith. We were all joined in a common cause. We did not look on government as something apart from the people. We thought of it as something to be used by the people for their own good.

New factory legislation setting up decent standards of safety and sanitation; limitation of the working hours of women in industry; a workmen's compensation law; a one-day-rest-in-seven law; a full train-crew law; a direct-primary law — these laws and many more were passed which were then called radical and alien to our form of government. Would you or any other Americans call them radical or alien today?

In later years, first under Governor Smith, then during my Governorship, this program of practical intelligence was carried forward over the typical and un-swerving opposition of Republican lead-ers throughout our State.

And today the great tradition of a lib-eral, progressive Democratic Party has been carried still further by your present Governor, Herbert H. Lehman. He has begun a program of insurance to remove the spectre of unemployment from the working people of the State. He has broadened our labor legislation. He has extended the supervision of public utility companies. He has proved himself an untiring seeker for the public good; a doer of social justice; a wise, conscien-tious, clear-headed and businesslike ad-ministrator of the executive branch of our Government. And be it noted that his opponents are led and backed by the same forces and, in many cases, by the same individuals who, for a quarter of a century, have tried to hamstring prog-ress within our State. The overwhelming majority of our citizens, up-state and down-state, regardless of party, propose to return him and his Administration to Albany for another two years.

His task in Albany, like my task in Washington, has been to maintain con-tact between statecraft and reality. In New York and in Washington, Govern-ment which has rendered more than lip service to our Constitutional Democracy has done a work for the protection and preservation of our institutions that could not have been accomplished by repres-sion and force.

Let me warn you and let me warn the Nation against the smooth evasion which says, "Of course we believe all these things; we believe in social security; we believe in work for the unemployed; we believe in saving homes. Cross our hearts and hope to die, we believe in all these things; but we do not like the way the present Administration is doing them.

Just turn them over to us. We will do all of them — we will do more of them — we will do them better; and, most important of all, the doing of them will not cost anybody anything."

But, my friends, these evaders are banking too heavily on the shortness of our memories. No one will forget that they had their golden opportunity — twelve long years of it.

Remember, too, that the first essential of doing a job well is to want to see the job done. Make no mistake about this: the Republican leadership today is not against the way we have done the job. The Republican leadership is against the job's being done.

Look to the source of the promises of the past. Governor Lehman knows and I know how little legislation in the in-terests of the average citizen would be on the statute books of the State of New York, and of the Federal Government, if we had waited for Republican leaders to pass it.

The same lack of purpose of fulfillment lies behind the promises of today. You cannot be an Old Guard Republican in the East, and a New Deal Republican in the West. You cannot promise to repeal taxes before one audience and promise to spend more of the taxpayers' money before another audience. You cannot promise tax relief for those who can afford to pay, and, at the same time, promise more of the taxpayers' money for those who are in need. You simply cannot make good on both promises at the same time.

Who is there in America who believes that we can run the risk of turning back our Government to the old leadership which brought it to the brink of 1933? Out of the strains and stresses of these years we have come to see that the true conservative is the man who has a real concern for injustices and takes thought against the day of reckoning. The true conservative seeks to protect the system of private property and free enterprise by correcting such injustices and inequalities as arise from it. The most serious threat to our institutions comes from those who refuse to face the need for change. Liberalism becomes the protection for the far-sighted conservative.

Never has a Nation made greater strides in the safeguarding of democracy than we have made during the past three years. Wise and prudent men — intelligent conservatives — have long known that in a changing world worthy institutions can be conserved only by adjusting them to the changing time. In the words of the great essayist, "The voice of great events is proclaiming to us. Reform if you would preserve."

I am that kind of conservative because I am that kind of liberal.

3. ADDRESS AT THE DEMOCRATIC VICTORY DINNER
WASHINGTON, D. C., MARCH 4, 1937

ON this fourth of March, 1937, in millions of homes, the thoughts of American families are reverting to the March 4th of another year. That day in 1933 represented the death of one era and the birth of another.

At that time we faced and met a grave national crisis. Now we face another crisis — of a different kind but fundamentally even more grave than that of four years ago. Tonight I want to begin with you a discussion of that crisis. I shall continue that discussion on Tuesday night in a nation-wide broadcast and thereafter, from time to time, as may be necessary. For I propose to follow my custom of speaking frankly to the Nation concerning our common problems.

I speak at this Victory Dinner not only as the head of the Democratic Party but as the representative of all Americans who have faith in political and economic democracy.

Our victory was not sectional. It did not come from compromises and bargains. It was the voice of twenty-seven million voters — from every part of the land.

The Democratic Party, once a minority party, is today the majority party by the greatest majority any party ever had.

It will remain the majority party so long as it continues to justify the faith of millions who had almost lost faith — so long as it continues to make modern democracy work — so long and no longer. We are celebrating the 1936 victory. That was not a final victory. It was a victory whereby our party won further opportunity to lead in the solution of the pressing problems that perplex our generation. Whether we shall celebrate in 1938, 1940, and in 1944, as we celebrate tonight, will deservedly depend upon whether the party continues on its course and solves those problems.

And if I have aught to say it will continue on its course and it will solve those problems.

After election day in 1936, some of our supporters were uneasy lest we grasp the excuse of a false era of good feeling to evade our obligations. They were worried by the evil symptom that the propaganda and the epithets of last Summer and Fall had died down.

Today, however, those who placed their confidence in us are reassured. For the tumult and the shouting have broken forth anew — and from substantially the same elements of opposition. This new roar is the best evidence in the world that we have begun to keep our promises, that we have begun to move against conditions under which one-third of this Nation is still ill-nourished, ill-clad, ill-housed.

We gave warning last November that we had only just begun to fight. Did some people really believe we did not mean it? Well — I meant it, and you meant it.

A few days ago, a distinguished member of the Congress came to see me to talk about national problems in general and about the problem of the Judiciary in particular.

I said to him:

"John, I want to tell you something that is very personal to me — something that you have a right to hear from my own lips. I have a great ambition in life."

My friend pricked up his ears.

I went on: "I am by no means satisfied with having twice been elected President of the United States by very large majorities. I have an even greater ambition."

By this time, my friend was sitting on the edge of his chair.

I continued: "John, my ambition relates to January 20, 1941." I could feel just what horrid thoughts my friend was thinking. So in order to relieve his anxiety, I went on to say: "My great ambition on January 20, 1941, is to turn over this desk and chair in the White House to my successor, whoever he may be, with the assurance that I am at the same time turning over to him as President, a Nation intact, a Nation at peace, a Nation prosperous, a Nation clear in its knowledge of what powers it has to serve its own citizens, a Nation that is in a position to use those powers to the full in order to move forward steadily to meet the modern needs of humanity — a Nation which has thus proved that the democratic form and methods of national government can and will succeed.

"In these coming years I want to provide such assurance. I want to get the nation as far along the road of progress as I can. I do not want to leave it to my successor in the condition in which Buchanan left it to Lincoln."

My friends, that ambition of mine for my successor can well be the serious ambition of every citizen who wants his United States to be handed down intact to his children and grandchildren.

I spoke in the dead earnestness of anxiety. I speak to you tonight in the same earnestness. For no one who sees as a whole today's picture of this Nation and the world can help but feel concern for the future.

To the President of the United States there come every day thousands of messages of appeal, of protest, of support, of information and advice, messages from rich and poor, from business man and farmer, from factory employee and relief worker, messages from every corner of our wide domain.

Those messages reflect the most striking feature of the life of this generation — the feature which men who live mentally in another generation can least understand — the ever-accelerating speed with which social forces now gather headway.

The issue of slavery, for example, took at least forty years — two generations — of argument, discussion and futile compromise, before it came to a head in the tragic war between the States.

But economic freedom for the wage earner and the farmer and the small business man will not wait, like emancipation, for forty years. It will not wait for four years. It will not wait at all.

After the World War, there arose everywhere insistent demands upon government that human needs be met. The unthinking, or those who dwell in the past, have tried to block them. The wise who live in the present have recognized their innate justice and irresistible pressure – and have sought to guide them.

In some countries, a royalist form of government failed to meet these demands – and fell. In other countries, a parliamentary form of government failed to meet these demands – and fell. In still other countries, governments have managed to hold on, but civil strife has flared or threats of upheaval persist.

Democracy in many lands has failed for the time being to meet human needs. People have become so fed up with futile debate and party bickerings over methods that they have been willing to surrender democratic processes and principles in order to get things done. They have forgotten the lessons of history that the ultimate failures of dictatorships cost humanity far more than any temporary failures of democracy.

In the United States democracy has not yet failed and does not need to fail. And we propose not to let it fail!

Nevertheless, I cannot tell you with complete candor that in these past few years democracy in the United States has fully succeeded. Nor can I tell you, under present circumstances, just where American democracy is headed nor just what it is permitted to do in order to insure its continued success and survival. I can only hope.

For as yet there is no definite assurance that the three horse team of the American system of government will pull together. If three well-matched horses are put to the task of ploughing up a field where the going is heavy, and the team of three pull as one, the field will be ploughed. If one horse lies down in the traces or plunges off in another direction, the field will not be ploughed.

What you and I call the principles of the New Deal did not originate on the fourth of March, 1933. We think of that date as their beginning, because it was not until then that the social demands they represented broke through the inertia of many years of failure to improve our political and economic processes.

What were those demands and needs? How far did we succeed in meeting them? What about them today?

Ever since the World War the farmers of America had been beating off evermounting disasters. This Administration tried to help them effectively where no other Administration had dared to take that risk.

The Agricultural Adjustment Act testified to our full faith and confidence that the very nature of our major crops makes them articles of commerce between the States.

The A.A.A. testified also to our full faith and confidence that the preservation of sound agriculture is essential to the general welfare – that the Congress of the United States had full constitutional authority to solve the national economic problems of the Nation's agriculture. By overwhelming votes, the Congress thought so too!

You know who assumed the power to veto, and did veto that program.

In the campaign of 1936, I said: "Of course we will continue our efforts in behalf of the farmers of America. With their continued cooperation we will do all in our power to end the piling up of huge surpluses which spelled ruinous prices for their crops. We will persist in successful action for better land use, for reforestation . . . for better marketing facilities for farm commodities, for a definite reduction of farm tenancy, for encouragement of farmer cooperatives, for crop insurance and a stable food supply. For all these things we have only just begun to fight."

Neither individually nor as a party can we postpone and run from that fight on advice of defeatist lawyers. But I defy anyone to read the majority opinion invalidating of the A.A.A. and tell us what we can do for agriculture in this session of the Congress with any reasonable certainty that what we do will not be nullified as unconstitutional.

The farmers were not the only people in distress in 1932. There were millions of workers in industry and in commerce who had lost their jobs, young people who had never been able to find their first job, and more millions whose jobs did not return them and their families enough to live on decently.

The Democratic Administration and the Congress made a gallant, sincere effort to raise wages, to reduce hours, to abolish child labor, to eliminate unfair trade practices.

We tried to establish machinery to adjust the relations between the employer and employee.

And what happened?

You know who assumed the power to veto, and did veto that program.

The Railroad Retirement Act, the National Recovery Act and the Guffey Coal Act were successively outlawed as the Child Labor Statute had been outlawed twenty years before.

Soon thereafter the Nation was told by a judicial pronunciamento that although the Federal Government had thus been rendered powerless to touch the problem of hour and wages, the States were equally helpless; and that it pleased the "personal economic predilections" of a majority of the Court that we live in a Nation where there is no legal power anywhere to deal with its most difficult practical problems — a No Man's Land of final futility.

Furthermore, court injunctions have paralyzed the machinery which we created by the National Labor Relations Act to settle great disputes raging in the industrial field, and, indeed, to prevent them from ever arising. We hope that this Act may yet escape final condemnation in the highest court. But so far the attitude and language of the courts in relation to many other laws have made the legality of this Act also uncertain, and have encouraged corporations to defy rather than obey it.

In the campaign of 1936, you and I promised this to working men and women:

"Of course we will continue to seek to improve working conditions for the workers of America — to reduce hours overlong, to increase wages that spell starvation, to end the labor of children, to wipe out sweatshops. . . . We will provide useful work for the needy unemployed. For all these things we have only just begun to fight."

And here again we cannot afford, either individually or as a party, to postpone or run from that fight on the advice of defeatist lawyers.

But I defy anyone to read the opinions concerning A.A.A., the Railroad Retirement Act, the National Recovery Act, the Guffey Coal Act and the New York Minimum Wage Law, and tell us exactly what, if anything, we can do for the industrial worker in this session of the Congress with any reasonable certainty that what we do will not be nullified as unconstitutional.

During the course of the past four years the Nation has been overwhelmed by disasters of flood and drought.

Modern science knows how to protect our land and our people from the recurrence of such catastrophes, and knows how to produce as a by-product the blessing of cheaper electric power. With the Tennessee Valley Authority we made a beginning of that kind of protection on an intelligent regional basis. With only two of its nine projected dams completed there was no flood damage in the valley of the Tennessee this winter.

But how can we confidently complete that Tennessee Valley project or extend the idea to the Ohio and other valleys while the lowest courts have not hesitated to paralyze its operations by sweeping injunctions?

The Ohio River and the Dust Bowl are not conversant with the habits of the Interstate Commerce Clause. But we shall never be safe in our lives, in our property, or in the heritage of our soil, until we have somehow made the Interstate Commerce Clause conversant with the habits of the Ohio River and the Dust Bowl.

In the campaign of 1936, you and I and all who supported us did take cognizance of the Ohio River and the Dust Bowl. We said: "Of course we will continue our efforts . . . for drought and flood control. . . For these things we have only just begun to fight."

Here, too, we cannot afford, either individually or as a party, to postpone or run away from that fight on advice of defeatist lawyers. Let them try that advice on sweating men piling sandbags on the levees at Cairo.

But I defy anyone to read the opinions in the T.V.A. case, the Duke Power case and the A.A.A. case and tell us exactly what we can do as a National Government in this session of the Congress to control flood and drought and generate cheap power with any reasonable certainty that what we do will not be nullified as unconstitutional.

The language of the decisions already rendered and the widespread refusal to obey law incited by the attitude of the courts, create doubts and difficulties for almost everything else for which we have promised to fight — help for the crippled, for the blind, for the mothers — insurance for the unemployed — security for the aged — protection of the consumer against monopoly and speculation — protection of the investor — the wiping out of slums — cheaper electricity for the homes and on the farms of America. You and I owe it to ourselves individually, as a party, and as a Nation to remove those doubts and difficulties.

In this fight, as the lawyers themselves say, time is of the essence. In three elections during the past five years great majorities have approved what we are trying to do. To me, and I am sure to you, those majorities mean that the people themselves realize the increasing urgency that we meet their needs now. Every delay creates risks of intervening events which make more and more difficult an intelligent, speedy, and democratic solution of our difficulties.

As Chief Executive and as the head of the Democratic Party, I am unwilling to take those risks — to the country and to the party — of postponing one moment beyond absolute necessity the time when we can free from legal doubt those policies which offer a progressive solution of our problems.

Floods and droughts and agricultural surpluses, strikes and industrial confusion and disorder, cannot be handled forever on a catch-as-catch-can basis.

I have another ambition — not so great an ambition as that which I have for the country, but an ambition which as a life-long Democrat, I do not believe unworthy. It is an ambition for the Democratic Party.

The Party, and its associates, have had the imagination to perceive essential unity below the surface of apparent diversity. We can, therefore, long remain a natural rallying point for the cooperative effort of all of those who truly believe in political and economic democracy.

It will take courage to let our minds be bold and find the ways to meet the needs of the Nation. But for our Party, now as always, the counsel of courage is the counsel of wisdom.

If we do not have the courage to lead the American people where they want to go, someone else will.

Here is one-third of a Nation ill-nourished, ill-clad, ill-housed — NOW!

Here are thousands upon thousands of farmers wondering whether next year's prices will meet their mortgage interest — NOW!

Here are thousands upon thousands of men and women laboring for long hours in factories for inadequate pay — NOW!

Here are thousands upon thousands of children who should be at school, working in mines and mills — NOW!

Here are strikes more far-reaching than we have ever known, costing millions of dollars — NOW!

Here are Spring floods threatening to roll again down our river valleys — NOW!

Here is the Dust Bowl beginning to blow again — NOW!

If we would keep faith with those who had faith in us, if we would make democracy succeed, I say we must act — NOW!

Herbert Hoover:

THE CHALLENGE TO LIBERTY

THE origins, character, and affinities of the Regimentation theory of economics and government, its impacts upon true American Liberalism, and its departures from it can best be determined by an examination of the actions taken and measures adopted in the United States during recent months.

It is not from oratory either in advocacy of this philosophy or equally in denial of it that we must search for its significance. That is to be found by an examination of the actual steps taken and proposed.

From this examination we may dismiss measures of relief of distress from depression, and reform of our laws regulating business when such actions conform to the domain of true Liberty, for these are, as I shall indicate, not Regimentation.

The first step of economic Regimentation is a vast centralization of power in the Executive. Without tedious recitation of the acts of the Congress delegating powers over the people to the Executive or his assistants, and omitting relief and regulatory acts, the powers which have been assumed include, directly or indirectly, the following:

To debase the coin and set its value; to inflate the currency; to buy and sell gold and silver; to buy Government bonds, other securities, and foreign exchange; to seize private stocks of gold at a price fixed by the Government; in effect giving to the Executive the power to "manage" the currency;

To levy sales taxes on food, clothing, and upon goods competitive to them (the processing tax) at such times and in such amounts as the Executive may determine;

To expend enormous sums from the appropriations for public works, relief, and agriculture upon projects not announced to the Congress at the time appropriations were made;

To create corporations for a wide variety of business activities, heretofore the exclusive field of private enterprise;

To install services and to manufacture commodities in competition with citizens;

To buy and sell commodities; to fix minimum prices for industries or dealers; to fix handling charges and therefore profits; to eliminate "unfair" trade practices;

To allot the amount of production to individual farms and factories and the character of goods they shall produce; to destroy commodities; to fix stocks of commodities to be on hand;

To estop expansion or development of industries or of specific plant and equipment;

To establish minimum wages; to fix maximum hours and conditions of labor;

To impose collective bargaining;

To organize administrative agencies outside the Civil Service requirements;

To abrogate the effect of the anti-trust acts;

To raise and lower the tariffs and to discriminate between nations in their application;

To abrogate certain governmental contracts without compensation or review by the courts;

To enforce most of these powers where they affect the individual by fine and imprisonment through prosecution in the courts, with a further reserved authority in many trades through license to deprive men of their business and livelihood without any appeal to the courts.

Most of these powers may be delegated by the Executive to any appointee and the appointees are mostly without the usual confirmation by the Senate. The staffs of most of the new organizations are not selected by the merit requirements of the Civil Service. These direct or indirect powers were practically all of them delegated by the Congress to the Executive upon the representation that they were "emergency" authorities, and most of them are limited to a specific time for the purpose of bringing about national recovery from the depression.

At some time or place all of these authorities already have been used. Powers once delegated are bound to be used, for one step drives to another. Moreover, some group somewhere gains benefits or privilege by the use of every power. Once a power is granted, therefore, groups begin to exert the pressure necessary to force its use. Once used, a vested interest is created which thereafter opposes any relaxation and thereby makes for permanence. But beyond this, many steps once taken set economic forces in motion which cannot be retrieved. Already we have witnessed all these processes in action.

The manner of use of these powers and their immediate impacts upon the concepts of true American Liberty may first be examined under the five groups or ideas into which they naturally fall – Regimented Industry and Commerce, Regimented Agriculture, Government in Competitive Business, Managed Currency and Credit, and Managed Foreign Trade.

Regimented Industry and Commerce

The application of Regimentation to business has made great strides. We now have the important branches of industry and commerce organized into trade groups, each presided over by a committee of part trade and part governmental representatives heading up through an "Administrator" to the Executive. There are a number of advisory boards for various purposes whose personnel is part trade and part bureaucratic. More than 400 separate trades have been so organized, estimated to cover 1,500,000 establishments or about 90 per cent of the business of the country outside of farming.

In this organization of commerce and industry the trades were called upon to propose codes of management for their special callings. Parts of each of these codes are, however, imposed by law, whether the trades propose them or not. The determination as to who represents the trade is reserved to the Executive, and in the absence of a satisfactory proposal he may himself make and promulgate a code. He may force deletion of any proposed provision and may similarly impose provisions and exceptions.

Each of the codes is directly or indirectly binding upon every member of the trade whether he was represented in its making or whether he agreed or not. It has the force of statutory law, enforceable by fine and jail through the courts. Originally the Executive could require every member of a trade to take out a license to do business. In this license he could impose the conditions under which persons may continue to do business. The Executive could revoke a license without affording any appeal to or protection of the courts. This licensing power has expired in general industry but still stands as an authority to the Secretary of Agriculture over all producers, processors and dealers in agricultural products. That is a very considerable part of American business. Except as an example of the extent of violation of freedom this licensing provision is not important, as the other provisions and methods are sufficiently coercive without it.

The codes impose minimum wages and maximum hours and provide, further, for collective agreement with labor as to wages and conditions of work beyond the minimums. By far the major use of the codes is, however, devoted to the elimination of "unfair competitive practices." This expression or its counterpart, "fair competition," has been interpreted not alone to cover "unethical" practices, but to include the forced elimination of much normal functioning of competition through reduced production, the prevention of plant expansion, and a score of devices for fixing of minimum prices and trade margins. From so innocent terms as "fair competition" and its counterpart have been builded this gigantic dictation — itself a profound example of the growth of power when once granted.

In this mobilization there has been constant use of the term "co-operation." However, the law itself makes important parts of the codes compulsory and by their indirect powers can impose any of them. As practical persons observing their working, we may dismiss voluntary impulses as the motivation of this organization. At best it is "coercive co-operation." Free will and consent, the essential

elements in co-operation, have not often been present. The spirit of the whole process has been coercive, principally through the overshadowing authority to impose the codes and the terror of effective deprival to any man of his business and his livelihood. The mere fact of charges made by bureaucrats can act to deprive him of his reputation. Where such authority arises among free men is difficult to discern.

Ample evidence of coercion is found in the bludgeoning proceedings of many important code conferences, in the changes forced in some codes, from which there was no appeal or refuge; in the incitement to public boycott; and in the contracts required in all dealings with the government itself. One need but read the vast flood of propaganda, of threat and pressure, the daily statements of the administering officials, and follow the actions of "compliance" boards and other agencies, in every town or village, to confirm the fact of coercion. Men have been fined or ordered to jail for the crime of selling goods or services at lower prices than their competitors. One of the sad results is the arraying of neighbor against neighbor, group against group, all grasping for desperate advantage from the law.

There are "unfair practices" which need reform because of the failure of some States to rise fully to their responsibilities. The codes have served admirably to reduce child labor by about 25 per cent, and they have eliminated sweating in certain trades. They have eliminated some unethical business practices, but they have stimulated many more new ones through "chiseling." This sort of reform is within the powers of the States, and laws to this purpose have been enacted by most of them. If we have determined that we must nationally force these measures on delinquent States and if they be within the constitutional powers of the Federal Government, then they can be carried out by specific law enforced by the judicial arm and do not require the regimentation of the economic system. But in practical working only a small part of the codes are devoted to these ends.

The most effective part of code operations are devoted to limitation of real competition. It is true that the law provided that there should be no monopolies or monopolistic practices. The major aspiration of those seeking to avoid the anti-trust acts always has been precisely the fixing of minimum prices and restriction of output, and these objectives, so earnestly yearned for in some quarters, now have been imposed by law. The economic results, so far as the trades and consumers are concerned, are about the same as if the anti-trust acts had been abolished. Naturally, if these industrial regiments hold to discipline they are at once constituted as complete guild monopolies as any in the Elizabethan period, from which we derived much of our American antagonism to monopoly.

But an equally regrettable social effect has been that the imposition of larger costs, and the fixing of minimum prices and trade differentials crashes down at once on smaller units of business. If persisted in there can be no destiny of these processes in the long run but a gradual absorption of business by the larger units. All this is in fact the greatest legal mechanism ever devised for squeezing the smaller competitor out of action, easily and by the majesty of the law. Yet the small business is the very fibre of our community life.

Over it all is now the daily dictation by Government in every town and village every day in the week, of how men are to conduct their daily lives — under constant threat of jail, for crimes which have no moral turpitude. All this is the most stupendous invasion of the whole spirit of Liberty that the nation has witnessed since the days of Colonial America.

Regimented Agriculture

The farmer is the most tragic figure in our present situation. From the collapse of war inflation, from boom, from displacement of work-animals by mechanization, from the breakdown of foreign markets, from the financial debacle of Europe, and from drought, he has suffered almost beyond human endurance.

Instead of temporarily reducing the production of marginal lands by measures of relief pending world recovery, the great majority of farmers were regimented to reduce production from the fertile lands. The idea of a subsidy to a farmer to reduce his production in a particular "staple commodity" was expanded by requiring a contract that he would follow orders from the Secretary of Agriculture in the production of other "staple commodities." Voluntary action was further submerged by threats that if he did not sign up he would have difficulty in obtaining credit.

The whole process has been a profound example both of how bureaucracy, once given powers to invade Liberty, proceeds to fatten and enlarge its activities, and of how departures from practical human nature and economic experience soon find themselves so entangled as to force more and more violent steps.

To escape the embarrassment of the failure to reduce production by these methods, still further steps were taken into coercion and regimentation. Yet more "staples," not authorized by the Congress to be controlled when the contracts were signed, were added to the list. A further step was to use the taxing power on excess production of cotton and to set quotas on sugar. Directly or indirectly, on many farms these devices create a privilege and destroy a right. Since only those who have had the habit of producing cotton and some other commodities may now do so, they are given a monopoly and any other farmer is precluded from turning his land to that purpose.

And recently still further powers were demanded from the Congress by which the last details of complete coercion and dictation might be exerted not alone to farmers but to everyone who manufactures and distributes farm products. That all this is marching to full regimentation of thirty millions of our agricultural population is obvious enough.

But we are told that the farmer must, in the future, sacrifice Liberty to economic comfort. The economic comfort up to date may be questioned, as likewise the longevity of any comfort, for the basic premise is not tenable.[1]

The stark fact is that if part of Liberty to a particular farmer is removed, the program must move quickly into complete dictation, for there are here no intermediate stages. The nature of agriculture makes it impossible to have regimentation up to a point and freedom of action beyond that point. Either the farmer must use his own judgment, must be free to plant and sell as he wills, or he must take orders from the corporal put above him.

The whole thesis behind this program is the very theory that man is

[1] Thomas Jefferson once said, "Were we directed from Washington when to sow, and when to reap, we should soon want bread." *Autobiography*, Vol. I, p. 113.

but the pawn of the state. It is a usurpation of the primary liberties of men by government.

Government in Competitive Business

The deliberate entry of the government into business in competition with the citizen, or in replacement of private enterprise, (other than as a minor incident to some major public purpose), is regimentation of the people directly into a bureaucracy. That, of course, is Socialism in the connotation of any sociologist or economist and is confirmed as such today by the acclaim of the Socialists.

As an instance we may cite the Tennessee Valley Authority, where the major purpose of the government is the purchase, construction, operation, transmission, and sale of electricity in the Tennessee Valley and neighborhood, together with the manufacture and merchandising of appliances, fertilizers, chemicals, and other commodities. Other instances occur where Public Works money has been allotted to the erection of dams and reservoirs, and to the construction of power plants, the major purpose of which is to undertake the production and sale of electricity in competition with the citizen.

There have long been instances of public works for the real major purpose of flood control, irrigation, or navigation, which produce water-power as a by-product. Here, if the government leases this power under proper protections to the public, the competition with the citizen is avoided. Here is one of the definite boundaries between Liberty and Socialism. Under Liberty, the citizen must have strong regulation of the rates and profits of power companies to protect him from oppression by the operator of a natural monopoly. But where the government deliberately enters into the power business as a major purpose in competition with the citizen — that is Socialism.

Still other instances of government competition with citizens are five corporations created by the government under the laws of Delaware, which are engaged in various competitive businesses covering the manufacture and merchandising of commodities.

These entries into Socialism were not an important emergency call to relieve unemployment. The total expenditures provided will employ but a very small percentage of the unemployed. In fact, the threat to private enterprise will probably stifle employment of more men in the damage to existing enterprises. There is already an ample private capacity to supply any of the commodities they produce, whether electricity, fertilizers, rum, or furniture. Whatever their output is, its production will displace that much private employment somewhere. We have only to examine a fragment of the statements of their sponsors to find that their purposes, although sometimes offered as employment, are in fact further blows pounding in the wedge of Socialism as a part of regimenting the people into a bureaucracy.

There are measures in banking and credit which might be discussed under this heading but they are dealt with elsewhere. And in another chapter of this book I have dealt at length with the effect and destiny of Socialism.

Managed Currency and Credit

The scope of this survey does not include a full examination of monetary, fiscal, and credit policies. I am here concerned solely with profound departures from Liberty.

Without entering upon the recent technical monetary steps taken, it may be said at once that the intent of the powers given to alter the unit value of currency is, by "managed currency," to enable the government to change from time to time the purchasing power of the currency for all commodities, wages, salaries, and income. One underlying intent of the monetary measures was the transfer of income and property from one individual to another, or from one group to another, upon an enormous scale without judicial processes. Whether the theory under this assumption will produce the effects intended or not, the intent is definitely expressed.

The installation of managed currency required the repudiation of the government contract to meet its obligations in gold.[2] And the repudiation of the gold clause extended much farther than repudiation of government obligations

[2] "Why are we going off the gold standard? With nearly 40 per cent of the entire gold supplies of the world, why are we going off the gold standard? With all the ear-marked gold, with all the securities of ours that they hold, foreign governments could withdraw in total less than $700,-000,000 of our gold, which would leave us an ample fund of gold, in the extremest case, to maintain gold payments both abroad and at home.

"To me, the suggestion that we may devalue the gold dollar 50 per cent means national repudiation. To me it means dishonor; in my conception, it is immoral.

"All the legalistic arguments which the lawyers of the Senate, men of eminent ability and refinement, may make here, or have made here, have not dislodged from my mind the irrevocable conviction that it is immoral, and that it means not only a contravention of my party's platform in that respect, but of the promises of party spokesmen during the campaign.

"Mr. President, there was never any necessity for a gold embargo. There is no necessity for making statutory criminals of citizens of the United States who may please to take property in the shape of gold or currency out of banks and use it for their own purposes as they may please. . . .

"If there were need to go off the gold standard, very well, I would say let us go off the gold standard; but there has been no need for that." — *From the Senate remarks of Mr. Glass, Senator from Virginia, April 27, 1933.*

alone, for it changed the value of all contracts between citizens far beyond the present appreciation of the citizen of its possible results — if it shall prove to have the effect which was intended.

One of the major objectives stated was to reduce unbearable debt. It was asserted that the value of the dollar as represented in its purchasing power for goods or services had changed from its value when the original bargains of debt were made. Under this operation the citizens were regimented into two groups, debtors and creditors. An empirical and universal amount of 40 to 50 per cent was set as the degree of shift in the value of all property to the debtor regiment from the creditor regiment.

This act involved the widest responsibility which the government bears to its citizens, and that individuals bear toward each other. For fidelity to contract, unless determined unconscionable by an independent tribunal, is the very integrity of Liberty and of any economic society. Where the debt of certain groups such as part of the farmers and home-owners becomes oppressive, and its social results to the entire nation are of vital importance, such a service is justified, but it should not have been undertaken at the particular cost of those honest creditors whose savings have been thus invested but should have been a special burden upon the whole nation. But the injustice is far wider than this.

These monetary acts extend the assumption of unbearable debt over the whole of the private and public debts of the nation. That this attempt at universal shift of 40 to 50 per cent of the value of all debts was neither necessary nor just can be demonstrated in a few sentences. The theory mistakenly assumed that the distorted prices and values at the depth of a banking panic were permanent. It assumed that the recovery from depres-

sion in progress through the world would not extend to the United States. Of even more importance, this theory also assumed that every single debt had become oppressive; that every single creditor had benefited by about one-half since the initial bargain; that every single debtor had lost by this amount; that no debtor could carry out his initial bargain; and that the respective rights of every debtor and every creditor in every kind of property should be shifted from debtor to creditor without any inquiry or process of justice. Debt is an individual thing, not a mass transaction. The circumstances of every debt vary.

Certainly the Government cannot contend that its debt was oppressive. No man has yet stated that the Government could not have paid its obligations in full. It was not insolvent. It was not bankrupt.

In large areas of private debt the borrower was amply able to meet his obligations. In other great areas he had already profited by large dividends or earnings, or otherwise by the use of the savings of lenders which he had deliberately solicited. A huge part of the bond issues of railways, of power companies, of industrial companies, of foreign governments, current commercial debt, the bank deposits, urban mortgages and what not belong to these categories.

The evidence of the volume of debts which require governmental relief as a social necessity does not by any conceivable calculation indicate more than a very minor percentage of the total public and private debt. Extensive provisions for the adjustment between individuals of their debts were made by new facilities under the bankruptcy acts and the further relief measures provided through the use of government credit.

But let us examine the injustice under this managed currency more particularly. In a great category where debt required adjustment there had already been many compromises between debtors and investors, as witness the many reorganizations of urban building loans, and corporate and other obligations, which were the products of inflation. The people's savings invested in these cases are required, by depreciation of the dollar, to submit to a still further loss.

Most lending is ultimately from savings which mean somebody's self-denial of the joy of spending today in order to provide for the future. But the borrower is often enough a person who secured these joys and is now to be relieved of part payment, although a large part of these borrowers are able to pay. The man who borrowed from an insurance company to build himself a more expensive and enjoyable house has secured these joys at the cost of the policyholder, who had hoped by self-denial to escape dependency. This applies equally to the huge debt of industrial and commercial businesses which profited by their borrowings from the policyholder and the depositor in a savings bank.

Those self-denying investors – the thrifty of the nation – who were willing to accept a low rate of interest in order to obtain the maximum security, are under this theory to have the purchasing value of their savings now shrunken in exactly the same ratio as the avaricious who received extortionate rates, or the reckless who took high risks. The holders of hard-won savings – the widow's mite – invested in 3¼ per cent first mortgage industrial bonds are called upon to sacrifice the same proportion as the holders of 7 per cent third mortgages. By the transfer of values from the first mortgage bondholder to the common stockholder the security of these speculative bonds is even increased. At once we see the evidence of this in the marked advance in the prices of these speculative debts. This disregard of prudence and this benefit to recklessness particularly penalizes a very large part of insurance and the great public endowment assets.

Ten billions of endowments in educational, hospitalization, and welfare activities – creditors whose debtors are mostly corporations and governments – are to be depleted in purchasing power. These endowed institutions give the leadership necessary to all our vast complex of public institutions. Yet if this theory eventuate, their activities must diminish by 40 per cent.

Furthermore, if this theory shall succeed, in the great bulk of industrial debt, the empirical reduction of purchasing power of the regiments of bondholders transfers this purchasing power to the regiments of common stockholders. Any inspection of who are the rank and file in these regiments will at once demonstrate the double injustice. The holders of bonds are largely the insurance company, the savings bank depositor, the small investor, and the endowed institution.

If this intent of devaluation shall eventuate, the transfer of property by government fiat from sixty million insurance policyholders to ten million stockholders is not even diffusion of wealth. It is further concentration of wealth. As a matter of fact, any survey of the total results would show (if the theory of these acts works out) that it will benefit the richest members of the community, because their property is, in the main, in equities. The hardship will fall upon the great mass of the people who are indirect holders of obligations through their savings in insurance, in savings bank deposits, as well as those who directly hold bonds and mortgages. That is, in our modern American economy the rich are more largely the holders of equities and those of moderate means more largely the holders of obligations. Thus the rich hereby become richer, the poor poorer.

Monetary shifts in their very nature are mostly irretrievable. There can be little turning back.

In "managed currency" — a power of government fiat over the values of wages, income, and property — we find many by-products from the invasion of Liberty. To some academic theorists the Commodity Dollar may be perfect. But for thousands of years the whole human race has esteemed gold as the final gauge of values. Whether the sign of the index number, which is the kernel of this branch of "planned economics," be theoretically a better gauge or not, the fact remains that gold is a matter of faith. Men will long delay full faith in an abstraction such as the commodity index, with its uncertainties of political manipulation or of Executive determination. This has a pertinent application today. Those people who are employed are heaping up their savings. Yet these potential investors have hitherto hesitated to loan their savings over a long period, not knowing with what they may be paid in years to come nor what their rights may be. The durable goods industries are dependent upon this investment in the form of long-term credits. At the same time the country has an accumulated need for a vast amount of homes and equipment. As these credits are much restricted, vast numbers out of work suffer the injustice of cruel delays in otherwise possible employment.

How far the Regimentation of banking and the government dictation of credit through various government agencies may extend is not yet clear. There are national stresses in which the government must support private financial institutions, but it is unnecessary for it to enter into competitive business to accomplish this. And lest the government step over the line into Socialism this support must be limited to activities where there is no competition, or so organized as ultimately to be absorbed into the hands of private ownership. The original Reconstruction Finance Corporation is an example of the former and the Federal Reserve Banks, the Home Loan Banks, the Federal Land Banks, of the latter. There are, however, some of the new financial agencies and some uses being made of the old agencies which forecast occupation beyond these fields, and threaten dictation as to who may and who may not have credit. The threat to farmers of withholding credit to force them to sign crop contracts with the government is a current example of possibilities.

The reduction of the independence of the Federal Reserve Board and the Farm Loan System to dependency upon the political administration, the provisions for appointment of officials in the banks by government agencies, and certain provisions in the new regulatory acts, all at least give enormous powers of "managed credit."

If the purpose of all these activities is to enable the government to dictate which business or individual shall have credit and which shall not, we will witness a tyranny never before contemplated in our history.

The wounds to Liberty — and to justice upon which Liberty rests — in these monetary actions and policies are thus myriad. It is again a specific demonstration of a social philosophy defensible only on the ground that the citizen is but the pawn of the state — the negation of the whole philosophy of Liberty. Executive power over the coin is one of the oldest components of despotism.

Managed Foreign Trade

There is another segment of National Regimentation into which these other segments immediately force us, and that is foreign trade. The whole theory of controlled domestic production and prices falls to the ground unless imports also are rigidly controlled. As managed industry and agriculture operate, the nation must be surrounded with barriers which insulate it from economic currents beyond its borders. Going off the gold standard theoretically raised most tariffs 40 per cent, and theoretically imposed that barrier against goods on the free list as well. The additions to tariffs by the amount of the processing taxes are further indications of the inexorable mounting of trade barriers under such a plan.

There can be no escape from constant international difficulties. These difficulties were great enough when the government made a fixed tariff upon 34 per cent of the imports based upon a simple proposal of differences in cost of production at home and abroad, and allowed 66 per cent of its imports to enter freely, and when it treated every nation alike. But when, in effect, it places barriers of one sort or another on the whole 100 per cent of imports by currency and exchange manipulation, when these barriers are to shift with every government-made price in industry, when they are to be made to vary by favor in trading with different nations, through reciprocal tariffs, then there is no doubt we also have joined in the world economic war already disastrously in progress. That economic war is steadily drying up the standards of living of the world, our own included, and it is drying up the outlets for human initiative. The hope of the world in an economy of plenty through the huge increase in productive power which science has given us threatens to be stifled by these processes of nationalism and regimentation.

Men can higgle with each other in the markets of the world and there is no ripple in international good-will, but when governments do the higgling, then the spirit of antagonism between peoples is thrice inflamed.

This brief survey of examples of experience up to this time is sufficient to make clear the definition and nature of National Regimentation and its progress in the United States. There are other channels in which our economic and social life is being regimented which could be developed. These instances are certainly sufficient to show that its very spirit is government direction, management, and dictation of social and economic life. It is a vast shift from the American concept of human rights which even the government may not infringe to those social philosophies where men are wholly subjective to the state. It is a vast casualty to Liberty if it shall be continued.

Earl Browder: WHAT FOLLOWS AFTER THE ROOSEVELT VICTORY

LET us ... [consider] what follows after the Roosevelt victory [i.e., his re-election in 1936]. The balloting on November 3 could be called "the great repudiation." The large majority of people were first of all voting against Hearst, against the Liberty League, against Wall Street, against Landon, against reaction, fascism and jingoism. That is the first and most important significance of the election. It was a smashing defeat for reaction. But, though defeated, the forces of reaction were not routed. They are reforming their lines for new attacks, preparing new methods to gain the same ends they sought in the election. Forced to drop their plans to challenge the validity of the election, which they clearly had in mind in expectation of a close vote, the reactionaries, faced with a tremendous majority for Roosevelt, suddenly turned an about face and began to make love to Roosevelt. Hearst, who the day before election denounced him in the same terms as he does the Communists, against whom he incites lynch law, suddenly found in Roosevelt the qualities of an Andrew Jackson of the twentieth century.

If Roosevelt wants support from them, the reactionaries tell the world, he can get all he wants, for a "sane" policy that will curb the "wild men" who got into Congress in the landslide, in far too large numbers for reactionary comfort. The de-feated reactionaries hoped to recoup their fortunes through the Democratic Right wing, through influencing Roosevelt, through splitting the Democratic Party, and through the Supreme Court.

The Communist Party sees in the overwhelming defeat of reaction in the elections a great opportunity for the forces of the People's Front to move forward, for labor to achieve some of its demands, for all of the oppressed to win improvements in their situation. But this cannot be done if we sit and wait for someone to bring things to us on a platter. It will not happen if the masses rely upon Roosevelt. Progress can only come if we use the opportunity for organization and struggle on a broader and more determined line than ever before.

Evidence that millions of workers understand this point is to be seen in the rising movement in various industries, in marine, steel, clothing, textile and others. These workers know that now is the favorable time to gain demands, but that without organization and struggle nothing will happen. There is a mounting mood of confidence and readiness to struggle. This is the mood that must be roused, stimulated and organized to drive the whole movement forward for the People's Front.

Of course, the Democratic Party leaders and Roosevelt want nothing of the kind. They want everyone to be quiet and wait for whatever the new Congress will bring them. The Democratic Party wants to restore good relations with its extreme Right wing and with the reactionaries generally and still continue to absorb all Farmer-Labor Party sentiment and prevent its crystallization.

The A. F. of L. Executive Council, instead of leading the labor movement forward, pulls back and condemns even such hesitant efforts as Labor's Non-Partisan League and the C.I.O.'s steel drive. It is ready to split the whole labor movement rather than permit progress.

The C.I.O. unions, while moving forward for industrial organization, are marking time politically, waiting for new developments instead of helping bring them about. The statement of Labor's Non-Partisan League after the elections sounded only the call to be alert and to be ready for a possible realignment in 1940, but there was not a word about helping create this realignment. We can by no means agree with this passive attitude but must point out that it is an obstacle to progress.

The employing class is naturally aware of the mounting spirit for struggle of the masses and they are trying to head it off. That is the significance of the large number of voluntary pay increases that have been announced since the elections.

Only the organization and struggle for the masses, independent of capitalist parties and politicians, will realize their demands and expectations, through Congress and outside of Congress, and prepare the way for greater concessions later on.

True, the masses have "great expectations," as the *New York Times* expressed it, as a result of the defeat of reaction. They believed in the promises made to them. They expect higher wages and lower hours, with protection of the right of collective bargaining and trade union organization. They expect adequate relief and public works to care for the eleven million unemployed; and they are in the mood for sharp struggle to achieve these. They expect the improvement of the old-age pensions and social security law, and their extension to the whole population. They expect the wiping out of sweat-shops and child labor. The Negroes expect some of the equality that Ickes talked to them about. The farmers expect more relief from their burdens. The young people expect further help from the government. The masses expect a curb to be placed on the usurped powers of the Supreme Court. They expect the United States to take an active part in preserving peace in the world. They expect greater civil liberties.

All of these great expectations constitute the mandate given to Roosevelt by the overwhelming majority of his 27,000,000 supporters. It is these great expectations which must be transformed into the moving force for the creation of the People's Front and the independent struggle and organization to realize these things.

The crushing defeat of the Republicans hastened the disintegration of the old two-party system. It brought closer the growing split of the Democratic Party, the party which united progressive and reactionary elements in the election, elements which cannot long continue in the same party. It strengthened all the progressive tendencies among the voting population. All these things improve and broaden the prospects for the building of the People's Front. We can say that these prospects are much better than ever before.

But at the same time, while improving and broadening the prospects for a national Farmer-Labor Party, this very progress brings about a temporary delay in the organizational unity of all these forces in a definite national organization. Now more than ever there is a fear among many progressives of prematurely forming such a party and thereby narrowing it down, leaving behind and outside serious forces which can be brought in a little later or in a different form.

We want to hasten the formation of a national Farmer-Labor Party as much as possible. It was the absence of such a party in the last elections which seriously held back the growth of labor's power. Even the national application of the tactic of the American Labor Party in New York would have been a great advance. The closest thing we got to a national concentration of the Farmer-Labor Party forces was the valuable but very limited Chicago Conference of May 30. This produced no effective organization but only a platform. The Chicago platform alone, however, by its stimulating effect on all local movements, proved the tremendous role that can and will be played by a really effective national united front of all the progressive movements and organizations. That is what we have in mind when we call for a national Farmer-Labor Party.

We must soberly estimate, however, the moods and trends among the broad progressive ranks. We must find the way to unite the movements already outside of and independent of the Democratic Party and Progressive Republicans together with those that are still maturing within the old parties, and not yet ready for full independence. This means that we must conceive of the People's Front on a broader scale than merely the existing Farmer-Labor Party organizations. We must conceive of it on a scale that will unite the forces in the Farmer-Labor Party and other progressives together

with those forces crystallized in some form or other but not yet independent of the old parties.

Our experience in Washington and California confirms the correctness of this judgment. There is not the slightest doubt that we were correct in establishing the united front of these movements which were not yet independent of the Democratic Party. The struggle to realize the mandate of the elections will still further broaden and crystallize those progressive movements. We cannot, like Norman Thomas, wash our hands of these growing movements and demand that they spring forth overnight fully grown and mature, before we will recognize and work with them. We must be ready to help them through birth pangs and nurture them through all the difficulties of infancy.

There cannot be a blue-print which will answer by formula how the People's Front is to develop uniformly throughout the country. We must study the real forces at work among the people and their relations concretely, and find a way acceptable to these progressive forces which will unite them on a state scale, and later nationally. This broader unity will have to, for a time, at least, include in most places forces outside and inside of the two old parties. This is a necessity at present for the development of the Farmer-Labor Party on a broad mass basis.

More than ever now, we must emphasize that in the People's Front, and in the existing Farmer-Labor Parties which already realize in part the People's Front, we are not trying to obtain a camouflage for the Socialist and Communist Parties. In the People's Front we must at all costs include non-socialist progressives who will for a longer or shorter time be the overwhelming majority. Our aim in the

People's Front is to organize the majority of the people in the shortest possible time, against the worst reactionaries and exploiters, and get the maximum possible control of the government in the hands of this progressive majority. And we must say that the results of the election showed, more than we ever saw before, the possibility of achieving this.

Roosevelt and his close supporters, of course, want to create the impression that the people already have achieved this goal through his re-election. This illusion if not fought against can become an obstacle to the further growth of the People's Front. It will be fully dispersed only in the course of struggle, in independent struggle on the economic and political field to realize the great expectation of the workers; first of all in the industries, in the fight for wages, hours and unionization, and, second, in the legislative assemblies of the states and the national congress in the fight for social and labor legislation.

We do not need to waste time, as some people do, in speculations as to whether Roosevelt will turn Right or Left, although our prediction of a Right turn by Roosevelt as expressed before election is being realized in the administration's relief policy today. From past experience we know that his course will be determined in its major aspects entirely by the course of the road. Roosevelt always tries to find the middle of the road. If the road turns right he turns right. If the road turns left, he will turn left. The road of national life will be determined not by Roosevelt's mind or tendency, but by the relationship of forces, by the independent struggle of the masses in the economic and political fields. A strong and successful movement to organize the mass production industries will change the course of government and of Roosevelt to the Left more than all the persuasive arguments in the world.

Likewise, we need not be afraid that the workers and farmers will win too much through Roosevelt and will thus dull their appetite for more and make them conservative. We must encourage the masses to win everything possible through the election victory of Roosevelt, showing them that this can only be done through organization and struggle, and through political independence from Roosevelt. We can be quite sure that every gain under these conditions will only sharpen their appetite for more, while having increased their knowledge and their power to gain more.

Neither do we need to speculate on the question as to whether on a national scale the People's Front will be realized only in the form of a Farmer-Labor Party, or through its combination with other forms of organization and struggle of the masses. It is sufficient at this moment to take note of the necessity in many states to work for a time at least also through broader and less definitely crystallized forms than the Farmer-Labor Party. What will finally come out on a national scale will to a large degree be determined by the relation of forces within the Roosevelt following, between reactionary and progressive trends and forces. A split in that following is sure to come, but its form on a national scale is still impossible to predict with certainty. In this struggle we will also participate, and we will have many difficult, complicated, and dangerous problems to solve in organizing and influencing the masses in the struggles that take place within the Democratic Party and in some progressive sections of the Republican Party.

Basil Rauch: LAUNCHING THE SECOND NEW DEAL: 1935

THE President's Annual Message to Congress on January 4, 1935, launched the Second New Deal. It announced a fresh start almost as if a new administration were being inaugurated. Achievements of the previous two years were dismissed perfunctorily: credit was taken for recovery only in the fields of agriculture, industrial production, and profits. Social justice was the new goal. Reform was declared to be inseparable from recovery. The ultimate human objectives of reform the President sought to rescue from the confusion of piecemeal efforts:

We find our population suffering from old inequalities, little changed by past sporadic remedies. In spite of our efforts and in spite of our talk, we have not weeded out the overprivileged and we have not effectively lifted up the underprivileged.

This did not mean that the "profit motive" would be destroyed; but its definition was fairly unorthodox:

By the profit motive we mean the right by work to earn a decent livelihood for ourselves and for our families.

The attitude towards more conventional definitions of the profit motive was made clear:

We have . . . a clear mandate from the people, that Americans must forswear that conception of the acquisition of wealth which, through excessive profits, creates undue private power over private affairs and, to our misfortune, over public affairs as well. In building toward this end we do not destroy ambition, nor do we seek to divide our wealth into equal shares on stated occasions. We continue to recognize the greater ability of some to earn more than others. But we do assert that the ambition of the individual to obtain for him and his a proper security, a reasonable leisure, and a decent living throughout life is an ambition to be preferred to the appetite for great wealth and great power.

Security of the men, women, and children of the nation was named as the central objective. A program was submitted to Congress designed to establish three types of security – "a program which because of many lost years will take many future years to fulfill." Stranded populations in the city and country should be rescued by better use of natural resources and intelligent distribution of means of livelihood. Unemployment and old-age insurance, benefits for destitute children, mothers, sick and physically handicapped persons should provide security against the major hazards of life. Housing was the third part of the program. Each of these problems of security had already been the subject of experimentation and comprehensive studies. But the President now gave up expectation that unemployment would be solved immediately by private enterprise and the NRA, and asked that it be dealt with in ways which would carry out the program for security. Recovery would be stimulated by the federal government pouring purchasing power into the hands of the least privileged groups, rather than by encouraging price rises which would increase profits and "seep down" in the form of higher wages to groups which would use their increased purchasing power to stimulate recovery. The shift from the latter program to the former, which was the shift from the First to the Second New Deal, was neither absolute nor sudden. The most practical justification for the change was the failure of the First New Deal, particularly NRA, to produce sound economic recovery, and the security program of 1935 was launched only after thorough experiment with the more conservative methods of achieving recovery.

The justification which the President offered for the new approach to unemployment was the "stark fact" that in spite of employment gains under NRA and the PWA program, approximately five million unemployed were still on the relief rolls. To continue to dole out relief to them would produce "spiritual and moral disintegration fundamentally destructive to the national fibre." The millions who were being attracted by the Townsend Movement, Father Coughlin's Social Justice, Huey Long's Share-Our-Wealth, and many other panaceas were perhaps in the President's mind when he spoke of saving "not only the bodies of the unemployed from destitution but also their self-respect, their self-reliance and courage and determination."

An estimated one and a half million who were on the relief rolls were unemployable. These the President wanted turned back to local agencies which would be assisted by federal social-security funds. The remaining group were employable, and Congress should establish a greatly enlarged and unified plan to provide employment for them by the federal government on projects such as slum clearance, rural electrification, and soil reclamation which would at the same time serve other purposes of the security program. The new work relief program would supersede FERA and all but a few normal public building operations of the PWA. Payment of the workers should be at a security wage level, higher than the existing dole but not so high as to discourage acceptance of private employment.

Besides the security program, the President suggested legislation to clarify and renew the National Industrial Recovery Act, strengthen anti-crime measures, reform public-utilities holding-company practices, and improve the forms and methods of taxation. Abnormal world conditions required continuation of acreage control in agriculture.[1]

The broad political significance of the launching of the security program of 1935 was that it ended the period during which the administration had supported economic policies of businessmen and established new ties of mutual support between the administration and all other groups of the population. The Message contained no invitation to businessmen to coöperate with the new program. By its nature they could have no imme-

[1] *Public Papers . . . of F. D. Roosevelt*, IV, 15–25.

diate effect upon its success or failure. Rather a warning was issued that speculative profits should not be sought or any action taken which would slow the program.

Many developments influenced the formulation of the new program. Dominant groups of businessmen had shown their determination to resist all compromise or coöperation with the administration when its policies had been drawn up partially by business leaders and were designed to benefit all groups equally. This resistance was climaxed by the organization and activities of the Liberty League which drew class lines across party divisions. Thus it could be said that issues of class interest and antagonism had been introduced not by the administration but by its opponents. The defeat of the Liberty League in the 1934 elections resulted in a new Congress which was eager to carry out an anti-business program as an inevitable consequence of the efforts of the League to override party divisions and elect Congressmen on grounds of class interest. If conservative Democrats abandoned their party in favor of a program which exclusively benefited property interests, the obvious strategy of the leaders of the Democratic Party was to design a program which should appeal more exclusively to farmers and laborers, and compensate for the loss of conservative support by winning over the minority of farmers and laborers who had remained loyal to the Republican Party.

The rise of the Committee for Industrial Organization, which brought employees of the great mass production industries into the labor movement and added a new militancy to it, also influenced the new orientation of the administration. The CIO and its aggressive leader, John L. Lewis, were determined to take advantage of the promises which had been made to labor during the early days of the NRA. They had fought the conservative unionism of the American Federation of Labor which was easily defeated by labor spying and company unionism in the mass-production industries. The refusal of businessmen to deal with organized labor had quickly disillusioned the CIO with the promises of businessmen and the administration, and it strove to end the tolerance by the administration all through 1934 of the refusal of businessmen to coöperate with the recovery program in ways favorable to labor. More broadly, the rise of a militant labor movement in the United States was contemporaneous with the suppression of the labor movement and the rise of reaction and fascism abroad, which led many Americans to welcome the growth of a powerful labor movement as a guaranty against the spread of fascism to the United States. Many leading American writers who had abandoned hope for the cultural and political health of their country during the period of reaction after the First World War were appalled by the ferocious forms which reaction assumed abroad. They began to rediscover the values of American democracy, and to work in sympathy with the labor movement to renovate and strengthen the institutions of democracy as protection against American reaction. Innumerable novels, dramas, and historical, economic, social, and political studies were published which expressed resurgent faith in American institutions and exposed the meaning and danger of reaction. The Second New Deal was synchronized with the new currents of American thought, and the growing ranks of liberals, who had been largely skeptical of, and even opposed to, the First New Deal, gave ardent support to the administration.

That the administration was lagging behind rather than leading the labor movement and resurgent liberalism was suggested by the limited scope of the security program as compared with the subsequent enactments of Congress. Several of the most important laws of the Second New Deal, including the Wagner Labor Relations Act and the Fair Labor Standards Act, were still opposed by the administration. The security program itself was eagerly and completely enacted by Congress. On January 17, the Social Security Bill was introduced and strongly recommended in a special message. The Bill looked to the states to assume responsibility for the relief of unemployables, but federal aid was offered to the states for this purpose and for health service agencies in proportion to the states' own appropriations. A federal tax on employers' payrolls, beginning at 1 and reaching 3 per cent in 1939 would build up funds for unemployment insurance. States which established approved insurance systems suited to local needs could receive and administer up to 90 per cent of the payments which employers within their borders had made. The remaining 10 per cent would be used to aid the states in meeting administrative expenses. The only feature of the Bill which would be exclusively federal was a plan for old-age pension insurance under which a tax of 1 per cent on both the wages of employees and the payrolls of employers would reach 3 per cent in 1949, and provide funds for pensions of from $10 to $85 per month for life for qualified employees who retired at 65.

Extensive hearings were held on the Bill. Most of the criticism came from those who considered it too limited in scope. The organized ranks of Dr. Townsend's Old Age Revolving Pension movement made a determined effort to substitute their scheme, which called for payments of $200 per month to the aged, to be derived from a universal 2 per cent tax on commercial transactions. The cost was estimated to be $20,000,000,000 per year, but since recipients would be required to spend their checks each month, it was expected that the depression would be incidentally cured. Townsend was put on the stand at the hearings on the administration Bill, not to provide a platform for him, but to discredit his movement by revealing the unsoundness of its theory, and by airing the squabbles among its leaders, the unsavory character of some of them as well as the private gains which they made from the contributions of their members. The motive was to turn the sincere followers of the Townsend movement against it and to attract them to the moderate program of the administration.

Spokesmen of the American Federation of Labor opposed the taxes on wages and payrolls, and proposed new taxes on incomes as the source of insurance funds. Many objections were made to the cutting down of purchasing power by taxes on wages. This argument was adopted by some conservative opponents of the Bill. President Emery of the National Association of Manufacturers declared that industry did not want to pay taxes for the social security of its employees. At the other extreme of opinion, Earl Browder, the head of the Communist Party, opposed the Bill on the ground that it was the responsibility of the wealthy alone to provide all funds needed for the relief of the unemployed, the aged, and other disadvantaged groups.[2]

[2] Senate Hearings: Committee on Finance (74th Congress: 1st Session), Vol. 15, pp. 922, 1217, et passim.

Supporters of the Bill found themselves in the position of moderates who refused to intensify radicalism by rejecting all proposals but made concessions which would minimize agitation for extreme measures. The only important difficulty over passage developed in a struggle between the Senate and the House for incompatible amendments. After a deadlock all amendments were abandoned except one to eliminate the administration's proposal that workers be allowed voluntarily to buy larger annuities than the compulsory pensions would provide. This amendment was a concession to private insurance companies which would have found the government competing with them for business.

The Social Security Act was passed in August and signed by the President with the statement that it did not provide complete protection against the "hazards and vicissitudes of life," but would give "some measure of protection to the average citizen," and by flattening out the peak of inflation and the valleys of deflation would lessen the force of possible future depressions and provide "an economic structure of vastly greater soundness."[3]

In his Annual Budget Message of January 3, the President requested that $4,000,000,000 be appropriated for giving work to employables on the relief rolls. This amount would be added to the national debt, all other expenses of the government being met by income. On January 24, he submitted the Reports of the National Resources Board and the Mississippi Valley Committee of the PWA, in order to demonstrate how relief work would be integrated with planned development of natural resources, especially land and water. In April, Congress appropriated funds, and

on May 6, the Works Progress Administration was established.

Harry Hopkins was made Administrator of the WPA, and as head also of the FERA, he had direct charge of transferring unemployables to local relief agencies and employables to the WPA projects. A Division of Applications and Information received suggestions for projects from any public or private source, and the Advisory Committee on Allotments transmitted plans to the President for approval and assignment of funds. The WPA utilized some forty existing administrative agencies of the federal government to organize projects which fell in their fields. Three important new agencies were organized: the Agricultural Resettlement, Rural Electrification, and National Youth Administrations. For smaller projects such groups were organized as the Federal Theatre Project, the Historical Records Survey, and many others. Some estimate of the variety and scope of WPA projects may be obtained from a random selection of a small fraction of its accomplishments during its first two years: 1,634 new school buildings, 105 airport landing fields, 3,000 tennis courts, 3,300 storage dams, 103 golf courses, 5,800 traveling libraries established, 1,654 medical and dental clinics established, 36,000 miles of new rural roads, 128,000,000 school lunches served, 2,000,000 home visits by nurses, 1,500 theatrical productions, 134 fish hatcheries, 1,100,000 Braille pages transcribed, and 17,000 literacy classes conducted per month.[4]

The great majority of WPA workers were unskilled laborers, but projects were organized whenever possible to use skilled and professional workers in activities for which they had been trained. Wages during the first year were paid

---

[3] *Public Papers . . . of F. D. Roosevelt*, IV, 324.   [4] *Ibid.*, V, 663–666.

on the "security" basis at a level higher than relief payments but lower than prevailing wages, and ranged from $15 per month for unskilled farm labor in the South to $90 per month for professional services in New York City. The objection that security wages encouraged private employers to lower their wage scales, especially after the invalidation of NIRA, led the administration in 1936 to raise the hourly rates on WPA projects to the prevailing level, but to reduce the number of hours worked per month so that the monthly totals remained at the security level.

The WPA was attacked through its stormy career from opposite viewpoints. Workers especially in the largest cities organized themselves into unions, of which the Workers' Alliance became the most militant. Even traditionally individualistic artists organized a union. These groups demanded the rights usually advocated by labor unions, especially representation on the administrative level, and on a few occasions conducted strikes against the WPA. The administration ruled that workers could not strike against relief of their economic distress, but efforts were made to receive and consider workers' proposals. These chiefly concerned details of administration and opposition to systems of discharging workers periodically. Failure to give work to all the eligible unemployed and frequent dismissals were also criticized. On the other hand, the WPA became a chief target of opponents of the administration. Charges of waste, coddling, and vote-getting motives became common. The WPA worker leaning on his shovel between rare dabblings in the dirt became a standard cartoon figure and the butt of innumerable jokes. Where labor efficiency could be measured, as on building projects, it was demonstrated that WPA labor was less productive than labor privately employed. To this the administration could answer that private employers had naturally dismissed their least efficient workers, and that the difference in cost between direct relief and the WPA program was more than repaid by the vast quantities of useful projects which were completed. And the use of work relief as a means of restoring purchasing power and achieving recovery seemed to be justified by the general prosperity which set in late in the summer of 1935 and suffered no relapses as had all previous upswings, for two years, after which the "recession" of 1937 followed the dismissal of the majority of WPA workers.

The Resettlement Administration was the response of the administration to the growing recognition that the AAA program did not aid, and in some respects injured, smaller diversified farmers, tenants, sharecroppers, and migrants. The main interest of the RA was in the farmers whose land was not productive enough to repay cultivation. The presence of over one million farm families on relief rolls had caused the FERA to undertake demonstration projects whereby submarginal land was purchased and devoted to forest, wild life, park, grazing, and other uses which were calculated to end erosion, restore productivity, and make the land socially useful. These projects were turned over to the RA and WPA labor was used on them. RA credits aided farmers from submarginal lands to resettle on productive land where their labor might become profitable. From the Department of the Interior, the Subsistence Homesteads Division was also taken over by the RA with its projects which were continued on a modified basis. Individual acreage was enlarged to provide a higher living standard, and the amortization period of loans was extended.

The RA also attacked the problem of farm tenancy, which had been growing at an alarming rate until over 40 per cent of all farmers had become tenants. Farms were bought by the RA and sold on easy terms to tenants selected for their character and ability. Various types of rehabilitation work were carried out, such as the granting of small emergency loans, assistance to groups of small farmers in buying heavy farm machinery on a co-operative basis, instruction in better farming methods, and assistance to young people to establish themselves as farmers. The most controversial activity of the RA was the creation of the Greenbelt Towns, which were experiments in planned suburban communities for low-income city workers. ˙Each community was built by WPA labor and designed for about seven hundred families as a village surrounded by a belt of farm and wood lands on which the residents could supplement their wages. A corporation of which all the villagers were members governed the town, paid taxes, and collected rents out of which it repaid to the government its investment. Only three communities were established in the vicinity of Washington, Cincinnati, and Milwaukee. These and the subsistence homestead communities, of which about thirty were organized, were storm centers of controversy. They were cited as proof that the administration harbored socialist or collectivist plans and wished to undermine individualism by regimentation and assertion of government responsibility. Those who sympathized with the experiments pointed to the free and self-governing institutions of the communities, the incentives to ambition

for better living which they provided, and their value as experiments for the possible solution of pressing economic and social problems.

An important criticism of the RA was that it encouraged the increase of agricultural production at a time when the AAA was seeking to reduce it in the interest of higher prices. In answer to this the President wrote:

> The task of resettling is to take farm families off . . . inferior land and move them to land where they can raise a fair proportion of the total national crop of any particular product. That total national crop, in turn, is so controlled by a crop-reduction program that a decent price may be obtained for all the farmers who have together produced that total. It is not that each resettled farmer is necessarily going to raise more crops on his new land than he did on his old. The important point is that when he does raise his share of the total crop, he is not compelled to lose money because of the difficulty and expense of making his bad land produce his farm products.[5]

The scope of the work of the RA was not sufficient to make it more than an experimental demonstration. After two years only 5,000,000 acres had been purchased, and 4,441 families had been resettled.[6] Cultivation of sub-marginal land and farm tenancy were only slightly affected, and sharecropping not at all. The Southern Tenant Farmers Union was organizing sharecroppers with some success, and it protested that the administration's major agricultural program, the AAA, was injuring all farm groups except the larger owners. The growing class of migrant farm laborers was the most distressed of all farm groups. The RA was

[5] *Public Papers . . . of F. D. Roosevelt*, IV, 152.
[6] *Ibid.*, pp. 149–151.

only an intermediate step towards the general solution of the problems of poorer farm groups, which was not undertaken until the Farm Security Administration was established in 1937.

The Rural Electrification Administration was established in May, 1935, to provide loans at low interest and WPA labor for the extension of power lines to farm homes where private utilities found too little opportunity for profit to undertake the investment. The sales of electrical appliances were expected to be stimulated by the REA program. Priority was given to projects which would distribute the power of publicly owned plants. In some areas conflicts developed between private companies whose owners feared the regulation of their rates which public ownership of power lines would make possible, and the REA projects. The threatened development of REA lines frequently stimulated the extension of power lines into rural districts by private companies and the lowering of their rates.

The National Youth Administration which was established in June, 1935, was intended to give to unemployed young people "their chance in school, their turn as apprentices and their opportunity for jobs — a chance to work and earn for themselves."[7] The problems of youth were particularly acute by 1935. Besides the obvious results of the depression, the NRA had caused industries to discharge about 1,500,000 workers of under 16 years, and minimum wage scales caused employers to give work to experienced laborers rather than to train apprentices. The Civilian Conservation Corps was expanded and placed under the WPA, but it gave work to only a half million boys at most, and none to girls. Early in 1935,

a survey showed that 3,000,000 people between 16 and 25 years of age were on relief, or one in every seven. Tens of thousands had left dispiriting homes and taken to roaming as tramps. Many turned to crime as a means of livelihood.

As an emergency measure the WPA established shelters to care for transient youths. The main object of the NYA was to return young people to schools and colleges and otherwise prepare them for socially constructive careers. In all cases work experience rather than direct relief payments was used to inculcate self-reliant habits. Schools and colleges were provided with funds and given control over their expenditure for part-time employment of students in clerical, library, laboratory, and other positions in the institutions. Vocational training, guidance, placement service, and apprentice agreements with private employers were organized by the NYA. Special PWA projects which would provide valuable work experience were developed for the employment and training of young people. By 1936, almost 600,000 were being reached at a given time by the various NYA activities. A striking feature was the participation of the young people themselves in the administration of the NYA, which was encouraged as training in citizenship.

During this period political organizations of youth, some of which were radical, attracted growing memberships, and a large number of them federated into the National Youth Congress. The latter organization attracted wide attention by its militant demonstrations against war and fascism and in favor of more thorough-going relief and reform policies by the government. Such activities sometimes caused more worry than did the problems which the depression had brought to youth, and led to the accusa-

[7] *Ibid.*, p. 281.

tion that the administration was coddling young people and nourishing class antagonisms. Supporters of the NYA argued that it gave to youth a practical demonstration of the creative and corrective powers of democracy and of the social value of work and self-help, which would compensate for the economic ills which made radical political solutions popular. If socialism attracted youthful supporters during these years, it was a remarkable fact that in the United States alone of all industrial nations, fascism won practically no adherents among young people.

The third part of the security program, "decent homes," was not made the subject of new legislation until 1937. In the meantime the activities of the Federal Housing Administration, first established in August, 1934, were expanded. Notes and mortgages for the repair and modernization of old and the construction of new homes and small business structures were insured by the FHA, so that a field which private bankers had not found profitable was entered by them on a large scale. The Housing Division of the PWA was retarded by the extreme caution which affected all PWA activities. A program of loans to limited-dividend corporations which would construct low-cost housing in slum districts was frustrated by the high cost of land, promotional schemes by private enterprises, and other factors, so that only 7 out of 533 contemplated projects were carried out. Direct federal construction of slum-clearing housing was largely prevented by the refusal of a Circuit Court in July, 1935, to admit the power of the government to exercise the right of eminent domain in acquiring slum properties. Early in 1936, the Comptroller General ruled that no subsidies but full economic rent must govern the rents charged tenants in the few projects which were being con-structed. The George-Healey Act was passed to authorize partial subsidies. Organization of local bodies which should construct slum-clearance projects with limited federal aid was encouraged and slowly realized. The difficulties which beset the housing program prevented any great progress until experience, growing public demand, and the Housing Act of 1937 finally made possible the provision of low-rent housing for appreciable numbers of slum dwellers in cities.

Besides the three proposals of the security program, improvement in the forms and methods of taxation had been asked for by the President in January, 1935. In June, he sent to Congress the famous special message on tax revision which was variously called a "soak-the-rich" scheme, an act of revenge on wealthy opponents of the administration, an attempt to reassert the administration's prestige after the first series of decisions of the Supreme Court invalidating New Deal laws, and a concession intended to draw to the administration the support of the members of Senator Huey Long's "Share Our Wealth" movement. The latter analysis of the significance of the message is possibly supported by internal evidence: "Social unrest and a deepening sense of unfairness are dangers to our national life which we must minimize by rigorous methods"[8] of ending favoritism to great wealth in taxation.

Senator Long had supported the administration only briefly after it came to power. He had opposed returning the banks to the control of their owners and other measures of the First New Deal, especially NIRA, which he considered a sell-out to Wall Street. His political machine in Louisiana began to suppress all

[8] *Ibid.*, p. 274.

opposition by methods which ranged from placing the election machinery in the exclusive control of Long appointees to the use of secret police. Complaints that liberty was being destroyed in Louisiana came to the White House, and the federal administration refused to turn Louisiana patronage over to the Long machine. In June, 1933, an interview with the President began with the Senator's refusal to take off his straw hat and proceeded through various types of offensive behavior and attempts to dominate the President. After it was over Long said to Postmaster General Farley: "What the hell is the use of coming down to see this fellow? I can't win any decision over him."[9]

The "Kingfish" thereupon went into total opposition to the administration, and used tactics of debate and filibuster to disrupt the administration's program in the Senate. He also organized the Share Our Wealth Society to win a personal following beyond the boundaries of his state. Local clubs were set up over a wide area, and the Senator engaged in an intensive campaign of appeals to less literate elements of the population, especially rural Southerners, with whom he had considerable success. Observers believed that his claim of March, 1934, was not unduly exaggerated: "Two hundred and fifty-four thousand earnest men and women are now dedicated to an unrelenting fight to divide up the wealth of this Land of Plenty so that children will not starve and their parents beg for crusts."[10] He demanded that the federal government guarantee an income of $5,000 per year to every family, thus making "Every Man a King."

This pill was sweetened for conservatives by "limitations" of private fortunes to $50,000,000, of legacies to $5,000,000, and of incomes to $1,000,000 per year. In this propaganda vicious attacks were made on Wall Street as the source of capitalist iniquities, and the administration was pictured as being its tool:

Black Sheep, Wall Street, have you any gold?
    Yes, sir; yes, sir; all I can hold.
Thanks to the New Deal I've made a billion
    more
    And I've stuck it all away in my little chain
    store.[11]

The significance of Long's anti-capitalism was indicated by the outcome of a conflict with oil companies in Louisiana. After raising threats to ruin the companies by taxation, the campaign was suddenly dropped after an alleged private deal between politicians and companies. Improvements of state roads, free textbooks in schools, free hospitals, and expansion of the University of Louisiana were pointed to as proof of the Senator's sincerity as a reform leader. But the graft with which later trials and investigations revealed state activities to be riddled suggested that his reforms were burdens to the people rather than improvements of their condition. The Long combination of captivating oratory and propaganda, impossible promises, unlimited corruption, and ruthless destruction of civil liberties in the interest of building a one-man political machine and wiping out all opposition made observers declare that it was the most dangerous of the native fascist movements of the period. Unlike the leaders of smaller groups, Long did not avow fascist doctrine: he was said to remark that in the United

[9] Farley, *Behind the Ballots*, p. 242.

[10] *The American Progress*, Vol. I, No. 32 (Mar. 29, 1934), p. 1.

[11] *Ibid.*, Vol. II, No. 3 (Feb. 1, 1935), p. 4.

States fascism would arrive in the guise of anti-fascism.

Long's feud with the administration became relentless. Department of Justice officials brought suit against members of the Long machine after finding evidence that they had failed to pay taxes on income from corrupt sources. Long worked to obtain personal control of federal-unemployment and work-relief funds allocated to Louisiana. Among other devices, the state legislature under his dictation enacted laws which would give the Governor and the Tax Board control over PWA loans. The motive was said to be not merely the desire for graft but unwillingness that any political, business, or unemployed opponents of the Long machine should benefit by federal funds. The national administration under these circumstances refused to make allotments for Louisiana, on the grounds that state control was not permissible under the federal laws governing the administration of funds, and that their distribution on the basis of need would be compromised. In the Senate, Long's fantastic tirades and filibusters against the administration made him notorious throughout the nation. His Share Our Wealth clubs grew to ominous dimensions by 1935. It was commonly expected that he would challenge the President for the Democratic nomination for the Presidency in 1936.

In the summer of 1935, Long established martial law in Louisiana and took complete control of the state as dictator in all but name. Secret police terrorized opponents and abolished judicial guaranties. Municipal government was reduced to subservience. Courts were subjected to limitations in procedure which made them ineffective. Taxes and appropriations and expenditures were no longer subject to audit. In September,

Long was assassinated by the son of an opponent, and the machine and dictatorship he had built up were gradually liquidated while the state made its peace with the federal government. Many of Long's henchmen were brought to trial. Others, like the Reverend Gerald L. K. Smith, cast about for new opportunities.

The Long movement had become of national importance within and outside the Democratic Party when the President issued his special message on taxation. At first Long praised the program in a letter to the President. He conceded that the wind had been taken out of his movement and that the Share Our Wealth clubs would support the President.[12] Later he thought better of his praise, and turned to strenuous opposition of the program on the ground that its terms were too moderate.[13]

The Presidential message asserted that "our revenue laws have operated in many ways to the unfair advantage of the few, and they have done little to prevent an unjust concentration of wealth and economic power."[14] The sources of modern wealth were declared to be not only personal thrift and industry but also speculation, the labor and coöperation of the masses of the population, and the advantages and protection which government confers upon corporations. The dominant purpose of tax revision should be the redistribution of tax burdens according to ability to pay. Higher taxes on inheritances and gifts were justified on the ground that taxation of "static wealth" would not disturb the mechanisms of production. Higher taxes on large individual incomes would reduce the "dis-

[12] *Current History,* Vol. 42 (Aug., 1935), p. 515.
[13] *The American Progress,* Vol. II, No. 8 (July, 1935), p. 1.
[14] *Public Papers . . . of F. D. Roosevelt,* IV, 271.

turbing effects upon our national life" of great wealth and carry out the "very sound public policy of encouraging a wider distribution of wealth."[15] The existing laws taxed an income of $5,000,000 at the same rate as one of $1,000,000, while a person with an income of $6,000 paid double the rate of one with $4,000.

Besides eliminating such inequities in individual income taxes, the principle of ability to pay should be extended to corporation tax rates. In place of the existing uniform corporation income tax of 13¾ per cent, the rate for smaller corporations might be reduced to 10¾ per cent, and the rates graduated to a level of 16¾ per cent on the highest corporation incomes. Such a system would be particularly fair because small corporations were more subject to state taxes and regulations than large corporations which were engaged in interstate commerce. To prevent evasion of the tax by the device of numerous subsidiaries and affiliates, a tax should be levied on dividends received by corporations. For later consideration the President suggested the elimination of unnecessary holding companies in all types of business, discouragement of unduly large corporate surpluses, a constitutional amendment to permit federal taxation of the income from subsequent issues of state and local government securities, and similar state powers over the income from federal issues.

A Wealth Tax Bill was written to carry out the President's recommendations, and it was debated in Congress largely in terms of the Long Share Our Wealth program. Long's opposition to the Bill because it was too moderate materially assisted in its passage, for his intransigence and unwillingness even to begin

with cautious measures were regarded as further proof of dangerous demagoguery. Conservative opposition to the Bill was stronger after it passed than before it became clear that a more extreme measure would not be substituted under the influence of Long. Congress installed minor changes in the Bill. Inheritance taxes were eliminated and estate taxes increased. Income tax rates for small corporations were only lowered to 12½ per cent and only increased to 15 per cent on all corporation incomes in excess of $50,000, but additional taxes were levied of 6 per cent on profits in excess of 10 per cent, and were graduated to 12 per cent on profits in excess of 15 per cent. Taxes on individual incomes above $1,000,000 were graduated steeply to 75 per cent on income in excess of $5,000,000. Holding companies which were used for the management of private fortunes were heavily taxed. The Wealth Tax Act was passed and signed on August 30.

Considerable public opposition to the Act developed on the ground that it was punitive. Roy W. Howard, owner of a chain of newspapers which had generally supported the administration, wrote to the President that businessmen who had once supported the New Deal were becoming increasingly hostile because they believed that the President had refused to broaden the tax base and had recommended the Wealth Tax measure in order to gain revenge on business rather than revenue. Business, he wrote, needed to have its fears allayed and a "breathing spell" from further experimentation. The President replied:

The tax program of which you speak is based upon a broad and just social and economic purpose. Such a purpose, it goes without saying, is not to destroy wealth, but to

15 *Ibid.*, pp. 273–274.

create broader range of opportunity, to restrain the growth of unwholesome and sterile accumulations and to lay the burdens of Government where they can best be carried. This law affects only those individual people who have incomes over $50,000 a year, and individual estates of decedents who leave over $40,000.

. . . Taxes on 95 percent of our corporations are actually reduced by the new tax law. . . .

Congress declined to broaden the tax base because it was recognized that the tax base had already been broadened to a very considerable extent during the past five years. . . .

. . . What is known as consumers' taxes, namely, the invisible taxes paid by people in every walk of life, fall relatively much more heavily upon the poor man than on the rich man. In 1929, consumers' taxes represented only 30 percent of the national revenue. Today they are 60 percent, and even with the passage of the recent tax bill the proportion of these consumers' taxes will drop only 5 percent.[16]

Then the President declared that the basic program to which the administration was pledged when it came to power "has now reached substantial completion and the 'breathing spell' of which you speak is here — very decidedly so."[17]

Less sympathetic businessmen than Roy Howard were appalled at the legislation passed during the 1935 session, and treated the "breathing spell" as a bad joke, for besides the security program and the Wealth Tax Act a series of laws to regulate business and to strengthen labor had been passed which were of major importance in the construction of the Second New Deal.

In March, the President strongly urged Congress to pass the Public Utility Holding Company Bill which had been writ-

[16] *Ibid.*, pp. 355–356.

[17] *Ibid.*, p. 357.

ten on the basis of special reports by the Federal Trade Commission and the National Power Policy Committee. The use of the holding company device during the twenties in order to exploit investors and to operate electric power and gas companies had become one of the major scandals of the period when public investigations and such incidents as the collapse of the Insull system revealed the methods which had been used. The abuses which the pyramiding of holding companies made possible were many. The purchase of a small amount of stock in an operating company by a holding company gave the directors of the holding company voting control over the operating company, and by assembling such control over great numbers of operating companies a holding company found that buyers would readily purchase its stock issues on the assumption dividends would rise with the economies which large scale organization would make possible. By raising tier upon tier of holding companies, which were related to other holding companies as well as to operating companies, an intricate web could be created which only the promoters, if anyone, understood, and high pressure methods could be used to unload endless series of stock issues on the public. Dividends were often falsified, being actually paid out of capital, and market prices rigged by pools. Commissions, legal fees, and other promotional profits could be saddled on the system with impunity. The high rates charged for electricity and gas to the public, and losses by investors ultimately paid for the exploits of the promoters. In 1925, holding companies controlled about 65 per cent of the electric power industry. By 1932, only the thirteen largest holding companies controlled 75 per cent of the industry. Natural-gas trunk pipe systems had been similarly centralized.[18] The resulting system of control of a vast industry by promoters who had made only slight investments, if any, the President in his message to Congress called "private socialism," and he declared that its destruction was essential if government socialism was to be avoided. The Bill recommended to Congress did not require the abolition of holding companies which performed demonstrably useful functions in terms of economies and efficiency of management; but a "death sentence" clause set a term of five years at the end of which any holding company which could not demonstrate its useful character would be forced to dissolve. The President declared that "except where it is absolutely necessary to the continued functioning of a geographically integrated operating utility system, the utility holding company with its present powers must go."[19] He drew particular attention to the vigorous campaign which the companies were waging against the Bill:

I have watched the use of investors' money to make the investor believe that the efforts of Government to protect him are designed to defraud him. I have seen much of the propaganda prepared against such legislation — even down to mimeographed sheets of instructions for propaganda to exploit the most farfetched and fallacious fears. . . .

Such a measure will not destroy legitimate business or wholesome and productive investment. It will not destroy a penny of actual value of those operating properties which holding companies now control and which holding company securities represent in so far as they have any value.[20]

18 *Ibid.*, p. 102.

19 *Ibid.*, p. 100.

20 *Ibid.*, pp. 98–99.

The "death sentence" caused a bitter fight which lasted through the session of Congress. The House deleted it when it first passed the Bill, but the Senate retained it. Both houses held investigations of charges that the utility companies and the administration were using extreme methods to bring pressure to bear on Congressmen. Administration leaders were accused of threatening Congressmen with the withdrawal of patronage. Tom Corcoran, an official of the RFC and intimate of the President, denied Representative Brewster's charge that the administration through Corcoran had threatened that it would stop the Passamaquoddy Dam Project in Brewster's state of Maine unless the Representative voted for the "death sentence." A former manager of a telegraph office testified that telegrams of protest against the Bill had been sent from his office over names taken by utility lobbyists from the telephone directory. The Senate found a record of $700,000 spent to oppose the Bill by one of the largest holding companies, the Associated Gas and Electric Company. Philip H. Gadsden, chairman of the main lobby organization, the Committee of Public Utility Executives, whose papers had been seized by the Senate committee, admitted that he had spent about $150,000 in creating sentiment against the Bill, and that in addition he had disbursed $150,000 in "lawyers' fees."[21]

The House was led to accept a Senate offer of compromise on the "death sentence" only after the President announced his willingness to accept the compromise also. The Act as it was signed on August 28 permitted two levels of holding companies above operating companies, but

21 *Current History*, Vol. 42 (Sept., 1935), p. 630.

otherwise maintained the "death sentence." The Securities and Exchange Commission was given power to regulate the financial practices of utility companies, and the Federal Power Commission received authority over the organizational provisions of the Act. After the new law was passed, utility companies largely disregarded it and depended upon the federal courts to come to their rescue by declaring the law unconstitutional. Over fifty suits were immediately instituted, and some lower federal courts upheld the companies. The Supreme Court ultimately upheld the constitutionality of the law.

The Motor Carrier Act and the Air Mail Act, which were signed in August, recognized the growth of competition with the railroads of bus, truck, and air transportation, and gave to the Interstate Commerce Commission powers to regulate rates, finances, and labor in the new fields which largely matched the powers it had long exercised over the railroads. The Banking Act of 1935, the Tennessee Valley Authority Amending Act, and the Gold Clause Act all clarified previous enactments. In May, Congress passed the Patman Bonus Bill, which called for inflation of the currency by issuance of greenbacks to the amount of $2,200,000,000 in order to pay war veterans immediately the full value of their adjusted service certificates which had been intended to mature in 1945. The President took the unprecedented step of delivering in person to a joint session of Congress a powerfully reasoned veto message. The veterans' lobby was not convinced, and the House overrode the veto, but the Senate sustained it by a narrow margin. The President's action was widely praised as evidence that he drew a sharp line against unsound infla-

tionary devices for increasing purchasing power even though this one gave him an opportunity to win the support of a powerful special interest group.

The Wagner-Connery Labor Relations Act, which was passed in 1935, was as important in the structure of the Second New Deal as the Social Security Act, but it was not in the strictest sense an administration measure. The refusal of the administration to accept it in 1934, and the change to a favorable attitude towards it after it was passed by Congress in July, 1935, was a significant aspect of the evolution of administration policy from the First to the Second New Deal, and was closely related to the decision to abandon the keystone of the First New Deal, the NIRA.

On February 20, 1935, the President recommended to Congress the extension of the NIRA for two years beyond its expiration in June, 1935. His request emphasized that the rights of labor under the law should be strengthened, and that the abuses of business should be curtailed:

We must make certain that the privilege of coöperating to prevent unfair competition will not be transformed into a license to strangle fair competition under the apparent sanction of the law. Small enterprises especially should be given added protection against discrimination and oppression.[22]

The message also cited the gains of labor under NRA, particularly the re-employment of about 4,000,000 people, the elimination of "the age-long curse of child labor," the outlawing of the sweatshop, and the release of millions of workers from starvation wages and excessive hours of labor. Business had gained from

[22] *Public Papers . . . of F. D. Roosevelt*, IV, 83.

the Act by being freed in part from dishonorable competition and destructive business practices and by safeguards for small enterprises. Consumers had gained by "less gouging in retail sales and prices than in any similar period of increasing demand and rising markets."[23]

But the President's favorable analysis of the effects of NIRA was poorly supported by the "Report on the Operation of the National Industrial Recovery Act," which was also made public in February by the Research and Planning Division of NRA. This report pointed out, for example, that payrolls in December, 1934, were only about 60 per cent of their level in 1926, while dividends and interest were 150 per cent of their total in 1926. The income of those who received interest and dividends was 50 per cent higher than in 1926, even though the national income was nearly 40 per cent lower and production had declined 33 per cent as compared with the earlier years.[24] Obviously, NIRA was not the only cause of the situation; but it had been intended to correct it. The President's new work relief program was also eloquent of the failure of NRA to accomplish what had been expected at its launching. By emphasizing the constructive achievements of the system and asking for modifications of the law which would expand them, the President indicated that he had not yet given up the original conception that the great majority of businessmen could be induced to coöperate with a planned recovery program with social objectives.

A Congressional investigation of NRA was already underway when the President sent his message. Most of the investigators were hostile to the experiment

from the liberal standpoint, and they concentrated on complaints against it rather than on the achievements which the President had summarized. Officials of the administration who appeared as witnesses admitted weaknesses of NRA, but asked for further opportunity to iron them out. Donald Richberg declared that "it is true that under some codes these [small] enterprises have suffered, but it is not true that the major effects of the codes have been injurious to small private enterprise."[25] William Green asked that the law be extended for two years even though labor had not obtained the benefits it expected, because the alternative was loss of the legal rights which organized labor had acquired. Defenders of the law pointed out that many of the recommendations of the Darrow Review Board had been put into effect and that the monopolistic tendencies of the first series of codes had been to some extent eliminated. Polls of the leading employers' organizations showed that members of the Chamber of Commerce favored continuation of NRA by almost three to one, while members of the National Association of Manufacturers opposed it by three to one.[26] General Hugh Johnson supported extension. He now admitted objections to the law, particularly that it promoted monopoly, which he had formerly denied and was inclined to agree they had been valid then; but that since his own "bad administration" had been ended, errors which he had made were in process of correction. He declared that the largest industries' leaders were divided between two views regarding the codes: some opposed them as restrictions on their freedom, while others

[23] *Ibid.*, p. 81.

[24] *Current History,* Vol. 42 (April, 1935), p. 66.

[25] *Senate Hearings: Committee on Finance* (74th Congress: 1st Session), Vol. 17, p. 14.

[26] *Ibid.*, pp. 127, 769.

believed that the system was inevitable and aimed to win control over it for themselves. Section 7A had substantially failed in its original purpose because of conflicting interpretations; clarification was the main need, and he was inclined to favor special legislation for that purpose. The General recommended: "Clean up NRA — don't destroy it. Let us scrub our infant offspring vigorously but let us not throw the baby down the drain pipe with the dirty water."[27]

In opposition to the proposal to extend NIRA, the advice of Kirton Varley on how to bring fascism to the United States was quoted from his book, *Gospel of Fascism:*

Study Italian practice in organizing the corporations and profit by the experience gained there. Organize the industrial organizations under the NRA administration into guilds with the same end in view.[28]

Considerable objection to NRA was made because it was based on the theory of economic scarcity. The chief tactic of the opponents of the law was to delay action by Congress until the Supreme Court should have handed down its decision on the constitutionality of the original Act. The administration, on the other hand, preferred to postpone tests until corrections in the law had been made.

The proposal to extend NIRA was also intended to prevent passage of the Wagner Labor Relations Bill and the Black Thirty Hour Bill, both of which were being pressed in Congress once more and by groups largely identical with the liberal and progressive opponents of NIRA. The Black Bill was being considered for the third time. Each time

it had become broader in scope, and now it covered virtually all industries and classes of wage earners. Senator Black offered it as a means of increasing purchasing power and of returning the unemployed to work in private industry. Representative Connery introduced it in the House. Through January and February, hearings were held which showed once more the division of opinion between businessmen who opposed such a drastic measure and labor leaders who approved it.[29] The Bill was successfully sidetracked. In spite of support by such progressive leaders as Senators Borah, LaFollette, and Norris, motion to consider the Bill in the Senate was defeated on April 8, largely by the votes of those who wished to wait until the question of NIRA renewal was settled.

The Wagner Labor Relations Bill was not so easily set aside. The Bill embodied the main provisions of the author's Labor Disputes Bill, which had been dropped at the President's request in 1934. The heart of the measure was the outlawing of employer-dominated company unions and the enforcement of the right of collective bargaining through representatives chosen by employees. Representative Connery introduced a similar bill of the same name in the House. Through the spring, the administration gave no support to the Wagner-Connery Bill, but labor made its strongest fight of the session for it. Extensive hearings in both houses were largely repetitious of hearings on the same proposal which had been held in 1934, but both sides presented their views with greater force. Again the National Association of Manufacturers and the industries which had organized company unions under NRA

[27] *Ibid.*, Vol. 18, p. 2454.

[28] *Ibid.*, Vol. 17, p. 1113.

[29] *Senate Hearings: Subcommittee of Committee on the Judiciary* (74th Congress: 1st Session), Vol. 14.

were the most aggressive opponents of the measure. The Liberty League took active part in the campaign. The chief argument of the opposition was that the Bill presupposed an unalterable antagonism between employers and employees, while company unions were founded on the principle of coöperation between the two groups, and on the actual mutuality of their interests. This argument was answered by pointing out that the Bill, on the contrary presupposed that the "class struggle" was not so inevitable that it could not be resolved by collective bargaining on the basis of mutual interests. Company unions which were financed and dominated by employers did not express the mutual interests of both classes, but the exclusive interests of the power that held the purse. Company unions which were not financed by employers would not be outlawed under the Bill. Employers already had their own organization in their management bodies: equality and mutuality could only be achieved by granting to labor the right to its organization, which must then have an opportunity to coöperate with the employer through collective bargaining. The argument that the leadership of labor unions was sometimes corrupt was answered by pointing out that some corporation managements had also been shown to be corrupt, particularly, as was revealed by the Senate investigation of civil liberties by the LaFollette Committee, in their anti-union activities; that such instances were not reasonable grounds for the refusal of labor unions to deal with management or management to deal with labor unions: checks on such practices were available to union members as to stockholders of corporations, short of infringements of public law which were subject to regular court proceedings.

The Bill declared that representatives chosen by the majority of workers in a particular factory unit should be the exclusive bargaining agents of all the workers in the unit. This clause aroused the particular support of labor leaders who recalled that the President had established the same principle in an Executive Order of February 1, 1934, and that on February 4, Johnson and Richberg for NRA had laid down the contrary rule, that representatives of a majority in a given unit could speak only for that group, while representatives of a minority could bargain with equal authority for its group, and that individuals could bargain for themselves, even to the point of making contracts containing different wage and other provisions. The opportunity which this rule gave to employers to break any union organization by granting better terms of employment to company union or non-union members, and, after union members had lost interest in their organization, changing to less favorable terms or refusing entirely to bargain, was described as an effective technique which was commonly used to evade the intent of the guaranty of collective bargaining which labor had received in NIRA. William Green said of the Johnson-Richberg rule:

This interpretation, I say to you, took the heart and teeth and soul out of Section 7(a); and we have never been able to overcome that interpretation because the administration itself never protested the interpretation.[30]

Senator Wagner stated a recent conference of the National Association of Manufacturers at White Sulphur Springs had

[30] *House Hearings: Committee on Labor* (74th Congress: 1st Session), Vol. 5, p. 203.

adopted a rule that when a majority of the members of a trade association agreed on a certain trade practice it would also bind the minority. This, he declared, was an example of the imposition of majority rule on business, while the same rule was denied to labor.

The growth of labor unrest and strikes was cited as proof that the spread of company unions and the emasculation of Section 7A did not solve the problems of labor relations. Most strikes grew out of the refusal of employers to recognize and bargain with an independent union even when it had a majority among the employees. While the hearings were going on, strike situations were developing in the automobile, rubber, and building service industries, each of which could be solved by recognition of an independent union. The lesson was made explicit by William Green:

I do not mind telling you that the spirit of the workers in America has been aroused. They are going to find a way to bargain collectively. The day of individualism is past, and they are tired of it, because they have been exploited. If they are denied the right to bargain collectively in an orderly way and through orderly processes, they are going to use their economic strength, and the American Federation of Labor will encourage them to use it, support them in using it. . . . The establishment of labor in our whole economic and political system in a place where it belongs must be recognized. Labor must have its place in the sun.[31]

To the Senate, Green made it plain that the AFL leadership was feeling the pressure of the growing militancy of the rank and file of labor: "We cannot and will not continue to urge workers to have patience, unless the Wagner bill is made

[31] *Ibid.*, p. 200.

law, and unless it is enforced, once it becomes law."[32] Francis Biddle, the chairman of the existing National Labor Relations Board, supported the new Bill as the solution of the problems which faced his Board. He also showed its connection with the general recovery program:

I think it is obvious that where labor is a party to and can bargain collectively, and with power behind the bargaining, that there is a greater chance for high wages; otherwise there would be no attempt to resist the burden by the employers. The real reason the employer resists this bill is because the employer knows it will increase purchasing power.[33]

The arguments of the opponents of the Bill were defensive, but the record of labor relations during the previous two years did not reflect favorably on the existing system. It became clear that the Bill was acquiring considerable support in Congress and among the public. Supporters of the Bill discussed at length the provision of the Connery measure in the House for a labor board within the Department of Labor as compared with the Wagner provision for an independent board whose members could not be removed except for cause. Secretary Perkins feared that an independent board would usurp the mediatory activities of the Department of Labor. Senator Wagner answered that he would not oppose the Secretary's plan if she were going to be Secretary of Labor forever, but since it would be necessary to pro-

[32] *Senate Hearings: Committee on Education and Labor* (74th Congress: 1st Session), Vol. 6, p. 122.

[33] *House Hearings: Committee on Labor* (74th Congress: 1st Session), Vol. 5, p. 174.

vide for the future, independence of judgment for personnel who exercised quasi-judicial functions could be permanently secured only by making the board free of Executive control. Wagner's view prevailed, and the House altered its Bill to suit the Senate version.

When the Bill reached the floor of the Senate, a last effort was made by Senator Tydings of Maryland to prevent it from favoring independent unionism. He offered an amendment which forbade coercion of employees by labor unions. This provision was presented as one which was required by fairness in order to match the ban on coercion by employers of their employees. It would have prevented organizational drives by independent unions to the same extent that employers were forbidden to urge their employees to join company unions. It would have changed the law from one which favored organized labor to one which would limit labor organizations to such as a group of employees in a particular factory could set up for themselves. A successful labor movement had not developed in any country under such conditions. It was the equivalent of forbidding organizational activities by employers' trade associations, or such "coercive" measures as the majority rule principle of the National Association of Manufacturers. The Tydings amendment was defeated on these grounds by a vote of 50 to 21 on May 16.

On May 14, the Senate had voted to extend NIRA for ten months. Senator Wagner was asked whether his Bill did not overlap the NIRA. The Senator was unwilling to oppose the administration's request for extension of NIRA, and he answered that his Bill defined the rights of labor more clearly than Section 7A and implemented them with provisions for enforcement: it would stand inde-

pendently of NIRA. At the same time the silence of the President was interpreted to mean that he was not yet ready to accept the Wagner-Connery Bill. On May 16, the liberals and progressives of the Senate, most of them Democrats, passed the Bill by an ample majority of 63 to 12.

Eleven days later the NIRA was declared unconstitutional by the Supreme Court in the famous "sick chicken" decision. This placed a new significance on the Wagner-Connery Bill. The administration indicated that it would ask for re-enactment of NIRA after changing its terms to meet the constitutional objections of the Court. But it never pressed for re-enactment aggressively, and ultimately it dropped the proposal entirely. In the meantime supporters of the Wagner-Connery Bill passed it through the House by a large majority.

Faced with the alternative of vetoing a bill which was strongly advocated by his own supporters within and outside of Congress, the President signed the Wagner-Connery National Labor Relations Act on July 5. It was the only important law of the whole New Deal period which the President had not initiated or at least advocated before its passage. But he supported the law strongly once it was passed, and by 1936 he was taking the lead in advocating re-enactment of the remainder of Section 7A, so that a wages and hours bill was passed in 1938 as the Fair Labor Standards Act.

The re-enactment in stronger form of the section of NIRA which was favorable to labor, coupled with the failure to re-enact the sections which were favorable to business, displays the evolution of policy away from the First New Deal and the major significance of the Second New Deal.

The passage of the Social Security Act, the WPA program, the Wealth Tax Act, laws subjecting public utility holding companies and new forms of transportation to federal regulation, and the National Labor Relations Act made the 1935 session of Congress perhaps the most important one in the field of domestic liberal-progressive reform in the nation's history. Labor supplanted farmers and business as the chief beneficiary of legislation for the first time.

But before the session had closed, the Supreme Court had shown that the whole structure of the New Deal, including the laws most recently enacted, was in danger of destruction at the hands of the conservative majority of the justices, and the greatest crisis of the administration was precipitated.

Arthur M. Schlesinger, Jr.:

THE BROAD ACCOMPLISHMENTS
OF THE NEW DEAL

The Crisis

Sullen men lived miserably in Hoovervilles, huddled against icy blasts, waited in grim lines for bread and soup, pondered a desperate march on Washington to collect bonus payments. Farmers, fighting bitterly against dispossession, moved toward open violence. Businessmen, stricken with panic, pleaded for government aid. Labor was disorganized and impotent. Intellectuals were clutching at Communism or at Fascism. And our national leadership? Clinging with frightened obstinacy to the theory that the forces which brought the depression would bring the revival, Herbert Hoover resisted the demand that the government act. It was the winter before the New Deal.

The election of 1932 presented America with one more chance to solve its problems democratically. Few considered Franklin Roosevelt a very strong or a very profound man; but the warmth and energy of his personality inspired confidence, and close observers could detect a new and bolder philosophy of government lurking behind the innocent generalities of his speech at the Commonwealth Club in San Francisco and behind such phrases as "the forgotten man" and "the New Deal." With his victory there began the resurgence of hope.

His debut — the bank holiday, the strong, ringing tones of the President, and the evaporation of fear — serves almost as a symbol of the Roosevelt policy. The cycle was to be repeated many times: stagnation and despair; a bold presidential stroke restoring hope; quick and spectacular action; and a conclusion which represented a substantial improvement but not a permanent solution. When Roosevelt finished with the banking crisis, the banks were established on a sounder basis than ever before in our history. Whether he might have taken the opportunity to nationalize the banking system is a question which used to exercise radicals in the middle thirties but which is perhaps based on a misunderstanding of Roosevelt's purposes.

First Phase of the New Deal

The hundred days thus began, with their brilliant, resourceful, and somewhat chaotic moves to prop up a crippled system — the start of a career of prolonged and ingenious improvisation. What else could there be but improvisation? Roosevelt, with his enlarged conception of governmental responsibility, had to face

From *Saving American Capitalism: A Liberal Economic Program*, Seymour E. Harris, ed., copyright 1948 by Alfred A. Knopf, Inc. Reprinted by permission of Alfred A. Knopf, Inc. This essay is a revision of an article first published in the *New Republic*.

problems without administrative precedent and without trained personnel, and
he had to act fast. No one knew better
than he the tentative character of his
program. "The country demands bold,
persistent experimentation," he had said
in the campaign. "It is common sense to
take a method and try it. If it fails, admit
it frankly and try another." This was to
be his rule (except for the part about
admitting failure frankly).

The Agricultural Adjustment Administration tried to solve the eternal farm
problem by curtailing crop production.
The Public Works Administration was set
up to expand purchasing power through
public works; under Harold Ickes's cautious management it remained free from
suspicion of graft at the price of a slow
start in its job of stimulating recovery.
The Works Progress Administration, providing work relief, became the great challenge to New Deal ingenuity. Though
some of its projects were correctly denounced as boondoggling, the total WPA
achievement was substantial, and its
contribution to cultural life rich and
varied.

In certain respects the National Recovery Administration was most significant for the future development of
the New Deal. In this experiment in
business self-regulation, the government
undertook to enforce codes of fair competition set up more or less by business itself.
In exchange, business accepted minimum
working hours, minimum wages, and
the abolition of child labor, and, above
all, Section 7A, with its guarantees for
collective bargaining.

In operation it soon became clear that
the big companies were running away
with the show. Exemption from anti-
trust prosecution led to happy public indulgence in such formerly secret vices as
price fixing and production quotas. While
Section 7A encouraged considerable honest labor organization, it was also diluted
in many cases to permit the formation of
company unions; and labor's bitterness
found expression in an outburst of strikes.
Moreover, though there was an upswing
in business, it did not look as if the NRA
was going to deliver the goods on employment and production. When the Supreme
Court bailed out the President by calling
the whole thing off in 1935, Roosevelt
wisely abandoned the experiment.

The failure of the NRA was accompanied by a growing bitterness toward
business and a basic redirection of the
New Deal. The change, which took place
late in 1934 and early in 1935, was signalized by the fall of the first brain trust
and the rise of a new set of presidential
advisers. When he first went to Washington, Roosevelt had surrounded himself
with men — Raymond Moley, Hugh Johnson, Donald Richberg — who shared the
belief that bigness was here to stay. These
men were convinced of the futility both
of trust-busting and of nationalization
and were seeking some means of stabiliz-
ing the economy through (in Moley's
phrase) "cooperative business-govern-
ment planning." Roosevelt had remarked
on signing the National Industrial Recovery Act, "It is a challenge to industry,
which has long insisted that, given the
right to act in unison, it could do much
for the general good which has hitherto
been unlawful. From today it has that
right."

And the result of business self-govern-
ment? Restrictions on production, chiseling of labor and of 7A, squeezing out of
small business, savage personal criticism
of the President, and the general tendency to trample down every one in the
rush for profits. Experience was teaching
Roosevelt what instinct and doctrine had
taught Jefferson and Jackson: that, to re-

form capitalism, you must fight the capitalists tooth and nail.

Roosevelt's new advisers – Ben Cohen, Tom Corcoran, Harry Hopkins, Harold Ickes – encouraged his natural tendencies to fight it out on a more liberal line. At the same time, the raucous activities of Huey Long and other pseudoradical prophets (Father Coughlin and Dr. Townsend), as well as the labor militancy stirred by John L. Lewis, showed the political necessity for a tack to the left. The result was the New Deal as we chiefly remember it – that determined, stalwart, eloquent fight against business domination, conducted by F. D. R. at his fighting best, backed by the loyal and alert intelligence of the New Dealers and by that weird coalition of city bosses, Southern Bourbons, trade unionists, liberal Republicans, Progressives and Farmer-Laborites, writers and intellectuals.

The attack on the Supreme Court, following Roosevelt's smashing victory in the 1936 elections, marked the high point of confident liberalism. The proposal to enlarge the court was itself disingenuous, cooked up in private jocularity and sprung without adequate preparation. Nevertheless the New Deal instinct to back the measure was probably correct, given the concrete situation. Recurrent attacks on the Supreme Court are an essential part of the physiology of our system; they constitute the natural and wholesome process by which the tissues of the court are restored before they are fatally overstrained.

One result was the court's change of heart and a constitutional green light for the New Deal. But the political price of even this partial victory was the alliance between the conservative Democrats and the Republicans. What Burt Wheeler joined together, Roosevelt could never

quite put asunder. The so-called purge of 1938 snapped further bonds of party loyalty; and the President's growing concern with the South as "the nation's No. 1 economic problem" warned the Southern Bourbons that new popular forces might be unleashed against them. Thus began that long and destructive guerrilla warfare which was to reduce the New Deal to practical impotence by the early forties.

This breaking up of the Democratic party was all the more unfortunate since it coincided with the gradual clarification of the New Deal economic program. The proscription of NRA enabled the New Dealers to clear the decks and begin anew on the problems of the American economy. This enterprise concentrated on two questions: recovery, and post-recovery economic organization.

Second Phase

During Roosevelt's first term, problems rained on the White House so furiously that the President could only improvise for short-term relief, not plan for long-term solutions. But, somewhere out of the welter of legislation, economic recovery received stimulus, and the curve of business activity began to go up. About this time Keynesian views of public spending were domesticated by Marriner Eccles and Alvin Hansen.

The President himself probably remained a balanced-budget man to the end, and Henry Morgenthau, Jr., his loyal Secretary of the Treasury, conducted a vigorous battle against the Keynesians – Ben Cohen, Leon Henderson and others – in 1937–38. But the recession of that winter, following the drastic cutbacks on spending in 1937, supplied the advocates of spending with a kind of circumstantial support; and the massive success of war spending in solving problems of production and employment appeared to demonstrate beyond reasonable doubt that you can stop the downward swing of the business cycle.

In its first formulation, the Keynesian program aimed at treating the problem of economic maturity; but it was later adapted to an attack upon the business cycle. Prosperity, it argued, depends on the maintenance of a high level of national income; and this high level, in turn, depends on the maintenance of capital formation and of purchasing power. Over-saving will cause a sag in both real investment and consumption and thus a sag in the national income. When such a decline begins, the government must offset the decrease in private spending by subsidizing capital formation and by subsidizing purchasing power.

The development of the anti-depression program was accompanied by a pretty thorough-going revision of NRA notions about American economic life. This process involved a restudy of the role of the concentration of economic power in restricting production. It was marked by the rise to dominance of people more or less in the Brandeis "anti-bigness" tradition (many of them brought to Washington by Felix Frankfurter): the lawyers Corcoran, Cohen, Landis, Douglas, Arnold, and the economists Henderson, Currie, and Lubin. It culminated in the appointment in 1938 of the Temporary National Economic Committee, whose conclusions are embodied in the TNEC monographs of 1940–41.

Roosevelt's terms of reference for the TNEC showed the great change from the days of the NRA. The NRA, he had said in 1933, "represents a supreme effort to stabilize for all time the many factors which make for the prosperity of the nation." But in 1938 he denounced interlocking financial controls for having taken away from American business "much of its traditional virility, independence, adaptability and daring." The basic TNEC thesis was "not that the system of free private enterprise for profit had failed in this generation, but that it has not been tried." The new effort aimed, not at stability, but at giving business incentives to take risks, expand production, and assume the main burden of maintaining the rate of real investment, all within an economy bounded by social security and by guaranteed rights for labor.

Achievements of the New Deal

By the time the TNEC conclusions were fully formulated, however, Roosevelt's attention had turned to a new and more urgent problem — the problem of the Axis war. For the rest of his life questions of strategy and diplomacy absorbed his attention; and, lacking his direct leadership, the New Deal itself transformed its character. All domestic issues were inevitably subordinated to the single goal of increasing war production. Toward the end, Roosevelt turned briefly to the domestic scene and indicated the directions in which he thought the New Deal should expand: government-guaranteed full employment, public housing, health insurance, enlarged social-security coverage, valley development, and a renewed anti-monopoly drive.

The New Deal had performed its necessary tasks well. It kept vital options open in American life. It faced up to an economic crisis that was widening rapidly into a moral and spiritual crisis, and it brought the country through, morally renewed and economically on a far sounder basis. Its accomplishments are so much a part of the landscape today that the twenties have acquired in retrospect the character of fantasy. Perhaps the best evidence of the extent to which the New Deal reshaped American ideas about society is to be found in the evolution of Republican platforms from 1932 to 1948. Perhaps the best evidence of the extent to which it healed the depression failure of nerve is to be found in the swift recuperation of the stricken American productive machine: a net national income which had fallen below 40 billion dollars in 1933 reached 74 billion in 1937 and 203 billion in 1947.

The immense expansion in productivity was accompanied by a far more equitable distribution of the national income, though marred by maldistribution induced by unemployment. An increasingly progressive tax structure served national economic policy by putting money into the hands of those who would spend it. The social-security system, and minimum-wage laws, the federal expenditures for welfare and relief, in addition to their obvious social functions, assisted the necessary economic task of maintaining purchasing power. Through the Wagner Act and related policies, moreover, the New Deal gave the labor movement power to fight for an increasing share in the national income.

The implications of the New Deal for the structure of the American economy are less clear cut. "The power of a few to manage the economic life of the nation," Roosevelt said in his instructions to the TNEC, "must be diffused among the many or be transferred to the public and its democratically responsible government." But the TNEC solution of anti-monopolism combined with social security and compensatory spending is not so simple as it sounds. The record certainly shows that existing anti-trust laws are inadequate to cope with the growing concentration of economic power; and, even if someone could devise an effective anti-monopoly program, the formula of free competition among small units in a social-security state would not by itself produce prosperity. The New Dealers made no fundamental attempt to grapple with the problem of the economies of concentration or of the decline in outlets for real investment.

The fact is that public spending, to be effective, will require a volume of capital formation which will rapidly bring government into new areas of economic activity. The question of the type of government activity then becomes acute. The European experience has corroded our faith (if, as followers of Jefferson, we ever had any) in the virtues of total state ownership; but the New Deal contribution to the exploration of other possibilities has been limited. In this light the TVA may be in the long run its most fruitful innovation. As a form of public ownership which does not conduce to economic or political centralization, the TVA provides a model to which officials seeking investment outlets for government funds will pay close attention. The U. S. A. is a vast country, and expenditures in valley development, public power, and conservation of natural resources can go far without having any effect on private capitalism except to invigorate it. There are other such noncompetitive outlets. Even Senator Taft has admitted that the free-enterprise system cannot provide adequate housing. The expansion of the social-security system, federal aid to education and for health, effective anti-inflation measures, and, above all, federal aid overseas under the European Recovery Program and its extension — all these provide means of keeping up demand which poach negligibly on the area of private enterprise.

Liberals must face the problem, however, that in another depression these outlets for government investment will not be enough. Can we then discover means of public spending which will not tend toward the establishment of oppressive public institutions or which will not rigidify and choke up the economy? Experience would suggest that we can go further than we have yet gone before the extension of government will mean the loss of essential liberties. The next generation will surely do a good deal of thinking about the problem of nationalizing basic industries — perhaps employing the device of the independent public corporation under a system of decentralization which would affect market incentives as little as possible. The experiments of Western Europe in democratic socialism may throw important light on the extent to which political freedom and state economic planning are compatible.

The great achievement of the New Deal was to introduce the United States to the twentieth century. Roosevelt redressed the defects of the Jeffersonian tradition by equipping the liberal party with a philosophy of government intervention — a belief, as he put it, that "the government has the definite duty to use all its power and resources to meet new social problems with new social controls." Much of the New Deal was imperfect, abortive, or ambiguous. Roosevelt's own administrative methods were insouciant, disorderly, and often demoralizing. But the shortcomings of the New Deal vanish in the general perspective of its supreme success: that is, in the restoration of America as a fighting faith, and in the restoration of democracy as a workable way of life.

The New Deal took a broken and despairing land and gave it new confidence in itself. Not perhaps new confidence; but rather a revival of the ancient faith in the free people which, speaking through Jefferson and Jackson and Lincoln, has been our great source of national strength. Roosevelt had a vision of democratic America and the strength to realize a good part of that vision. All his solutions were incomplete. But then all great problems are insoluble. The New Deal left us the fighting spirit and the broad democratic faith in which we may strive to advance the solutions a few steps further.

Richard Hofstadter: FRANKLIN D. ROOSEVELT: THE PATRICIAN AS OPPORTUNIST

WHEN the task of conducting a presidential campaign fell upon him, Roosevelt's background of economic innocence was dappled by only occasional traces of knowledge. "I don't find that he has read much about economic subjects," wrote Raymond Moley in a family letter April 12, 1932. "The frightening aspect of his methods is FDR's great receptivity. So far as I know he makes no efforts to check up on anything that I or anyone else has told him." On occasion his advisers were astounded by his glib treatment of complicated subjects. Once when his campaign speeches on the tariff were being prepared, and two utterly incompatible proposals were placed before him, Roosevelt left Moley speechless by airily suggesting that he should "weave the two together." That "great receptivity" which frightened Moley, however, was the secret of Roosevelt's political genius. He became an individual sounding-board for the grievances and remedies of the nation, which he tried to weave into a program that would be politically, if not economically, coherent.

Roosevelt's 1932 campaign utterances indicate that the New Deal had not yet taken form in his mind. He was clear on two premises: he rejected Hoover's thesis that the depression began abroad, insisting that it was a home-made product, and he denounced Hoover for spending too much money. He called the Hoover administration "the greatest spending Administration in peace time in all our history." The current deficit, he charged, was enough to "make us catch our breath." "Let us have the courage," he urged, "to stop borrowing to meet continuing deficits." And yet he was "unwilling that economy should be practiced at the expense of starving people." Still, he did not indicate how he proposed to relieve starving people. Public works? They could be no more than a "stopgap," even if billions of dollars were spent on them. He was firm in ascribing the depression to low domestic purchasing power, and declared that the government must "use wise measures of regulation which will bring the purchasing power back to normal." On the other hand, he surrendered to Hoover's idea that America's productive capacity demanded a large outlet in the export market. "If our factories run even 80 percent of capacity," he said (quite inaccurately),[1] "they will turn out more products than we as a nation can possibly use ourselves. The answer is that . . . we must sell some goods abroad."

Roosevelt made several specific promises to the farmers. There was one aspect of Hoover's farm policies that made him

---

[1] "The United States," concluded the authors of *America's Capacity to Consume*, "has not reached a stage of economic development in which it is possible to produce more than the American people as a whole would like to consume."

especially bitter — the attempt of the Farm Board to organize retrenchment in production, which Roosevelt called "the cruel joke of advising farmers to allow twenty percent of their wheat lands to lie idle, to plow up every third row of cotton and shoot every tenth dairy cow." His own program involved "planned use of the land," reforestation, and aid to farmers by reducing tariffs through bilateral negotiations. Later he backtracked on the tariff, however, promising "continued protection for American agriculture *as well as* American industry."

All Roosevelt's promises — to restore purchasing power and mass employment and relieve the needy and aid the farmer and raise agricultural prices and balance the budget and lower the tariff and continue protection — added up to a very discouraging performance to those who hoped for a coherent liberal program. The *New Republic* called the campaign "an obscene spectacle" on both sides.

Roosevelt delivered one speech at the Commonwealth Club in San Francisco, however, which did generally foreshadow the new tack that was to be taken under the New Deal. In this address Roosevelt clearly set down the thesis that the nation had arrived at a great watershed in its development. Popular government and a wide continent to exploit had given the United States an unusually favored early history, he asserted. Then the Industrial Revolution had brought a promise of abundance for all. But its productive capacity had been controlled by ruthless and wasteful men. Possessing free land and a growing population, and needing industrial plant, the country had been willing to pay the price of the accomplishments of the "ambitious man" and had offered him "unlimited reward provided only that he produced the economic plant so much desired." "The turn of the tide came with the turn of the century."

As America reached its last frontiers, the demand of the people for more positive controls of economic life gave rise to the Square Deal of Theodore Roosevelt and the New Freedom of Woodrow Wilson. In 1932 the nation was still faced with the problem of industrial control.

A glance at the situation today only too clearly indicates that equality of opportunity as we have known it no longer exists. Our industrial plant is built; the problem just now is whether under existing conditions it is not overbuilt. Our last frontier has long since been reached, and there is practically no more free land. More than half of our people do not live on the farms or on lands and cannot derive a living by cultivating their own property. There is no safety valve in the form of a Western prairie to which those thrown out of work by the Eastern economic machines can go for a new start. We are not able to invite the immigration from Europe to share our endless plenty. We are now providing a drab living for our own people. . . .

Just as freedom to farm has ceased, so also the opportunity in business has narrowed. . . . The unfeeling statistics of the past three decades show that the independent business man is running a losing race. . . . Recently a careful study was made of the concentration of business in the United States. It showed that our economic life was dominated by some six hundred odd corporations who [*sic*] controlled two-thirds of American industry. Ten million small business men divided the other third. More striking still, it appeared that if the process goes on at the same rate, at the end of another century we shall have all American industry controlled by a dozen corporations, and run by perhaps a hundred men. Put plainly, we are steering a steady course toward economic oligarchy, if we are not there already.

Clearly, all this calls for a re-appraisal of values. A mere builder of more industrial plants, a creator of more railroad systems, an organizer of more corporations, is as likely to be a danger as a help. The day of the great promoter or the financial Titan, to whom we granted anything if only he would build, or develop, is over. Our task now is not discovery or exploitation of natural resources, or necessarily producing more goods. It is the soberer, less dramatic business of administering resources and plants already in hand, of seeking to reestablish foreign markets for our surplus production, of meeting the problem of underconsumption, of adjusting production to consumption, of distributing wealth and products more equitably, of adapting existing economic organizations to the service of the people. The day of enlightened administration has come. . . .

As I see it, the task of government in its relation to business is to assist the development of an economic declaration of rights, an economic constitutional order. . . .

Happily, the times indicate that to create such an order not only is the proper policy of Government, but it is the only line of safety for our economic structures as well. We know, now, that these economic units cannot exist unless prosperity is uniform, that is, unless purchasing power is well distributed throughout every group in the nation.

In cold terms, American capitalism had come of age, the great era of individualism, expansion, and opportunity was dead. Further, the drying up of "natural" economic forces required that the government step in and guide the creation of a new economic order. Thus far Roosevelt had left behind the philosophy of his 1929 Tammany Hall speech. But in the Commonwealth Club speech two different and potentially inconsistent lines of government action are implied. One is suggested by the observation that the industrial plant is "overbuilt," that more plants will be "a danger," that production must be "adjusted" to consumption; the other by phrases like "meeting the problems of underconsumption," making pros-

perity "uniform," distributing purchasing power, and "an economic declaration of rights." The first involves a retrogressive economy of trade restriction and state-guided monopoly; the second emphasizes social justice and the conquest of poverty. In 1931 the United States Chamber of Commerce's Committee on Continuity of Business and Employment had declared in terms similar to Roosevelt's: "A freedom of action which might have been justified in the relatively simple life of the last century cannot be tolerated today. . . . We have left the period of extreme individualism." The committee then proposed a program very closely resembling the NRA as it was adopted in 1933. It is evident that Roosevelt's premises, far from being intrinsically progressive, were capable of being adapted to very conservative purposes. His version of the "matured economy" theory, although clothed in the rhetoric of liberalism and "social planning," could easily be put to the purposes of the trade associations and scarcity-mongers. The polar opposition between such a policy and the promise of making prosperity uniform and distributing purchasing power anticipated a basic ambiguity in the New Deal.

At one of his earliest press conferences Roosevelt compared himself to the quarterback in a football game. The quarterback knows what the next play will be, but beyond that he cannot predict or plan too rigidly because "future plays will depend on how the next one works." It was a token of his cast of mind that he used the metaphor of a game, and one in which chance plays a very large part. The New Deal will never be understood by anyone who looks for a single thread of policy, a far-reaching, far-seeing plan. It was a series of improvisations, many adopted very suddenly, many contradictory. Such unity as it had was in political strategy, not economics.

Roosevelt had little regard for the wisdom of economists as a professional caste. "I happen to know," he declared in his third fireside chat, "that professional economists have changed their definition of economic laws every five or ten years for a long time." Within the broad limits of what he deemed "sound policy" — and they were extremely broad limits — he understood that his administration would not be politically durable unless it could "weave together" many diverse, conflicting interests. He had built a brilliantly successful career in the Democratic Party on his flair for reconciling or straddling antagonistic elements, and he was too practical to abandon a solid bedrock of political harmony in favor of some flighty economic dogma that might be abandoned in "five or ten years." Frances Perkins tells how Lord Keynes, whose spending theories were influential with some New Deal economists, paid a brief visit to the President in 1934 and talked about economic theory. Roosevelt, bewildered at Keynes's "rigamarole of figures," told his Secretary of Labor: "He must be a mathematician rather than a political economist." Keynes for his part was somewhat disappointed, remarking that he had "supposed the President was more literate, economically speaking." The Britisher's mistake is likely to become a model for Roosevelt legend-makers.

Raymond Moley, in his *After Seven Years,* has compiled a fairly long but not exhaustive enumeration of the sharp swerves and tacks in Rooseveltian policy. It will be more simple and profitable to speak only of the two New Deals that were foreshadowed in the Commonwealth Club speech. In a sense both of them ran concurrently; but it is roughly accurate to say that the first was domi-

nant from Roosevelt's inauguration to the spring and summer of 1935 and that the second emerged during that period and lasted until the reform energies of the nation petered out.

The first New Deal, the New Deal of 1933–4, was conceived mainly for recovery. Reform elements and humane measures of immediate relief were subsidiary to the organized and subsidized scarcity advocated by the Chamber of Commerce, the Farm Bureau Federation, and the National Grange, and incarnated in the NRA and AAA. These great agencies, the core of the first New Deal, representing its basic plans for industry and agriculture, embodied the retrogressive idea of recovery through scarcity.

The AAA was the most striking illustration of organized scarcity in action. Although successful in raising farm prices and restoring farm income, it did just what Roosevelt had found so shocking in Hoover's Farm Board. To the common-sense mind the policy seemed to have solved the paradox of hunger in the midst of plenty only by doing away with plenty. In an address at Atlanta, in November 1935, Roosevelt implicitly conceded that the whole policy was geared to the failure of the American economy. He pointed out that the average American lived "on what the doctors would call a third-class diet." If the nation lived on a first-class diet, "we would have to put more acres than we have ever cultivated into the production of an additional supply of things for Americans to eat." The people lived on a third-class diet, he said candidly, because they could not afford to buy a first-class diet.[2]

2 The Ever Normal Granary Plan, enacted in 1938, was widely hailed as a more satisfactory policy. Although it promised greater price stability and other benefits, it still involved familiar plans for marketing quotas and the shadow of

The mainspring of the first New Deal was the NRA, which Roosevelt called "the most important and far-reaching legislation ever enacted by the American Congress . . . a supreme effort to stabilize for all time the many factors which make for the prosperity of the nation." Under it business received government sanction for sweeping price agreements and production quotas and in return accepted wage stipulations improving the condition of many of the poorest-paid workers.[3] It is not unfair to say that in essence the NRA embodied the conception of many businessmen that recovery was to be sought through systematic monopolization, high prices, and low production.[4] In spite of the enthusiasm with which its "planned" features were greeted, it retarded recovery, as the Brookings economists concluded, and a strong, sustained advance in business conditions began only after the Supreme Court killed it in May 1935.[5] Roosevelt was nevertheless slow to give up the NRA idea. In February 1935, asking for a two-

abundance still hung over it. Its sponsor, Henry Wallace, admitted that "several years of good weather" and good crops would "embarrass" the government.

[3] It may be necessary to say that NRA was not a universal business policy. A poll taken in 1935 showed that Chamber of Commerce members were almost three to one for continuing NRA, while NAM members opposed it three to one.

[4] NRA Administrator Hugh Johnson declared in an early press conference: "We are going to ask something in the nature of an armistice on increased producing capacity, until we see if we can get this upward spiral started. . . . We are going to plead very earnestly . . . not to use any further labor-saving devices or anything further to increase production for the present."

[5] The end of NRA was certainly not the only factor in the recovery that began in the summer of 1935, but it is beyond argument that the most sustained period of economic advance under the New Deal took place in the two years after the Blue Eagle was laid to rest.

year extension, he said that to abandon its "fundamental purposes and principles . . . would spell the return of industrial and labor chaos."

The initial New Deal was based upon a strategy that Roosevelt had called during the campaign "a true concert of interests," and that meant in practice something for everybody. Farmers got the AAA. Business got the NRA codes. Labor got wage-and-hour provisions and the collective-bargaining promise of Section 7(a). The unemployed got a variety of federal relief measures. The middle classes got the Home Owners' Loan Corporation, securities regulation, and other reforms. Some debtors were aided by inflation. As new discontents developed they were met with new expedients.

Despite all Roosevelt's efforts, however, the nation insistently divided into right and left, and his equivocal position became more difficult to maintain. Pressure from the organized and enheartened left became stronger; but Roosevelt was also baited into a leftward turn by die-hard conservatives. He was surprised and wounded at the way the upper classes turned on him. It has often been said that he betrayed his class; but if by his class one means the whole policy-making, power-wielding stratum, it would be just as true to say that his class betrayed him. Consider the situation in which he came to office. The economic machinery of the nation had broken down and its political structure was beginning to disintegrate. People who had anything to lose were frightened; they were willing to accept any way out that would leave them still in possession. During the emergency Roosevelt had had practically dictatorial powers. He had righted the keel of economic life and had turned politics safely back to its normal course. Although he had adopted many novel, perhaps risky expedients, he had avoided vital disturbances to the interests. For example, he had passed by an easy chance to solve the bank crisis by nationalization and instead followed a policy orthodox enough to win Hoover's approval. His basic policies for industry and agriculture had been designed after models supplied by great vested-interest groups. Of course, he had adopted several measures of relief and reform, but mainly of the sort that any wise and humane conservative would admit to be necessary. True, he had stirred the masses with a few hot words about "money changers" and chiselers, but he had been careful to identify these as a minority among businessmen. It was, after all, not Roosevelt but the terrible suffering of the depression that had caused mass discontent, and every sophisticate might be expected to know that in such times a few words against the evil rich are necessary to a politician's effectiveness.

Nothing that Roosevelt had done warranted the vituperation he soon got in the conservative press or the obscenities that the hate-Roosevelt maniacs were bruiting about in their clubs and dining-rooms. Quite understandably he began to feel that the people who were castigating him were muddle-headed ingrates. During the campaign of 1936 he compared them with the old man saved from drowning who berated his rescuer for not salvaging his hat — and again with a patient newly discharged from the hospital who had nothing but imprecations for his physician. Before 1935 Roosevelt had engaged in much political controversy, but he had generally managed to remain on friendly terms with his opponents. Surrounded from childhood with friendship, encouragement, and indulgence, he might have been able to accept criticism offered in the spirit of good-natured banter or

the proposal of constructive alternatives (which he would simply have appropriated), but the malice and deliberate stupidity of his critics made him angry, and his political struggle with the "economic royalists" soon became intensely personal. Professor Moley, who in 1932 had admired his lack of "a bloated sense of personal destiny," was saddened to hear him say in 1936: "There's one issue in this campaign. It's myself, and people must be either for me or against me." In public he grew aggressive. He would like to have it said of his second administration, he stated, that in it "the forces of selfishness and of lust for power . . . met their master."

The development of Roosevelt's relation to the left is of critical importance to the Roosevelt legend. Perhaps no aspect of his public relations has been so quickly forgotten as his early labor policy. At the beginning of his administration Roosevelt was an acquaintance, not a friend, of organized labor. Although he was eager to do something about the poorest-paid workers through the NRA codes, his attitude toward unions themselves was not overcordial. The NRA itself had been rushed into shape partly to head off the strong pro-labor provisions of the Black-Connery bill. Section 7(a) of NRA, which guaranteed the right of collective bargaining, did not ban individual bargaining, company unions, or the open shop. Workers at first rallied to the NRA with enthusiasm and entered the more aggressive unions by the thousands in response to the plausible but false appeal: "The President wants you to join." But when disputes arose under Section 7(a), General Hugh Johnson and Donald Richberg handed down interpretations that, in the language of the Brookings Institution economists, "had the practical effect of placing the NRA on the side of anti-union employers in their struggle against the trade unions. . . . The NRA thus threw its weight against labor in the balance of bargaining power." Roosevelt stood firmly behind his administrators. Further, his last appointee as NRA administrator was a notorious foe of labor, S. Clay Williams. By early 1935, when there were few in the ranks of organized labor who had any expectation of help from the White House, workers were calling the NRA the "National Run Around." On February 2 William Green threatened that the entire labor movement would oppose Roosevelt.[6]

In the meanwhile another political threat was arising. Huey Long, who had achieved the position of a major leader of mass opinion in the hinterland through his demagogic "share-the-wealth" movement, was talking about a third party. In his *Behind the Ballots* James A. Farley recalls that the Democratic National Committee, worried about the 1936 election, conducted a secret national poll to sound Long's strength. They were dismayed at what they learned. "It was easy to conceive a situation," reports Farley, "whereby Long . . . might have the balance of power in the 1936 election." Democrats also had private reports that he would be well financed if he ran. By mid-spring Professor Moley was horrified to hear Roosevelt speak of the need of doing something "to steal Long's thunder."[7]

It was at this point that the Supreme Court broke the mainspring of the original New Deal by declaring the NRA unconstitutional. Roosevelt, looking forward to 1936, now found himself in a difficult position. The Court had torn up his entire program for labor and industry. Labor seemed on the verge of withdrawing political support. Huey Long's popularity showed the dissatisfaction of a large part of the electorate. And no sign of a really decisive turn toward business recovery had yet come. The result was a sharp and sudden turn toward the left, the beginning of the second New Deal.

In June 1935 two striking measures were added to the President's list of "must" legislation: the Wagner labor-disputes bill and a drastic new "wealth tax" to steal Long's thunder. By the end of the 1935 legislative session the original New Deal, except for the AAA, was scarcely recognizable. In place of the NRA codes and the masquerade of Section 7(a) there was now a Labor Relations Board with a firm commitment to collective bargaining. A strong holding-company act and a stringent wealth tax stood on the books. None of these measures as they were finally enacted had been contemplated by Roosevelt at the beginning of the year. In the WPA a new relief program had been organized, with larger expenditures and a better wage scale. A Social Security Act had been passed. And at the close of the year the chief executive told Moley he was planning a "fighting speech" for his next annual message to Congress because "he was concerned about keeping his left-wing supporters satisfied."

Roosevelt's alliance with the left had not been planned; it had not even grown; it had erupted. The story of the Wagner Act, the keystone of his rapprochement with labor, and in a sense the heart of

---

[6] An article in the New York *Times*, February 3, 1935, under the heading, "LABOR UNIONS BREAK WITH THE NEW DEAL," reported that labor leaders were "almost in despair of making headway toward union recognition in the face of powerful industrial interests and an unsympathetic administration."

[7] The Townsend old-age pension movement was a menace of comparable importance, although it had not taken political form.

the second New Deal, is illustrative. The Wagner Act had never been an administration measure. It had been buffeted about the legislative chambers for more than a year without winning Roosevelt's interest. His Secretary of Labor recalls that he took no part in developing it, "was hardly consulted about it," and that "it did not particularly appeal to him when it was described to him." Nor did he altogether approve of the vigorous way in which it was later administered by the NLRB. Miss Perkins recalls that he was "startled" when he heard that the Board had ruled that no employer was to be able to file a petition for an election or ask the Board to settle a jurisdictional dispute. Yet under the stimulus of recovery and the protection of the NLRB, unions grew and flourished and provided the pressure in politics that gave the second New Deal its dynamic force. "A good democratic antidote for the power of big business," said Roosevelt.

Since Roosevelt was baited and frustrated by the right and adopted by the left, his ego was enlisted along with his sympathies in behalf of the popular point of view. During the formative period of the second New Deal he seems to have begun to feel that his social objectives demanded a crusade against the "autocracy." Early in 1936 at a Jackson Day dinner he made an elaborate and obvious comparison between Jackson and himself in which he observed of Jackson's hold on the common people: "They loved him for the enemies he had made." It is doubtful whether, even in Jackson's day, there had ever been such a close feeling of communion between a president and the great masses of the people as in the 1936 campaign. One incident that Roosevelt recalled for reporters touched him especially. He was driving through New Bedford, Massachusetts, when a young

girl broke through the secret-service guards and passed him a pathetic note. She was a textile worker. Under the NRA she had received the minimum of eleven dollars a week, but had recently suffered a fifty per cent wage cut. "You are the only man that can do anything about it," her note ended. "Please send somebody from Washington up here to restore our minimum wages because we cannot live on $4 or $5 or $6 a week."[8] Here was common ground: the "resplendent economic autocracy" that imposed such a pitiful wage scale was the same interest that was flaying the President. Without design by either, and yet not altogether by accident, Roosevelt and the New Bedford girl had been thrown together in a league of mutual defense.

Roosevelt's second inaugural address was a lofty and benign document in which he remarked with satisfaction on the improvement of "the moral climate of America," declared that the proper test of progress is "whether we provide enough for those who have too little," and called attention to "one-third of a nation, ill-housed, ill-clad, ill-nourished." In the first two years of his second administration he sponsored, in addition to the controversial Supreme Court reform bill, four new reform measures of broad economic importance: the Housing Act of 1937, the Fair Labor Standards Act, the Farm Security Act, and an unsuccessful proposal to set up a national string of seven TVA's. But the New Deal was designed for a capitalistic economy that, as Miss Perkins says, Roosevelt took as much for granted as he did his family. For success in attaining his stated goals of prosperity and distributive justice he was fundamentally dependent upon re-

[8] See Roosevelt's *Public Papers*, V, 624.

storing the health of capitalism. The final part of the New Deal story can be told not only in political battles and reform legislation but in jagged movements on the business-cycle graphs.

Early in 1937, administration circles, watching the rapid rise of the business index almost to 1929 levels, became fearful of a runaway boom. Federal Reserve officials put a brake upon credit, Roosevelt called upon Congress for economies, and WPA rolls were sliced in half. Roosevelt had never publicly accepted spending as a permanent governmental policy; although he had operated upon yearly deficits, he had always promised that when the national income reached a satisfactory level he would return to balanced budgets. But events proved that he had become a prisoner of the spending expedient. As Alvin Hansen has characterized it, the 1935–7 upswing was a "consumption recovery," financed and spurred by huge government outlays. When government expenditures were cut, a sharp downward trend began, which reached alarming dimensions early in 1938. Just at this time the National Resources Committee, an executive fact-finding agency, placed upon the president's desk a careful survey of consumer incomes for 1935–6. The committee estimated that 59 per cent of the families in the land had annual cash incomes of less than $1,250, 81 per cent less than $2,000. When this report reached him, Roosevelt knew that business conditions had again declined. There were still about 7,500,000 workers unemployed. Plainly something fundamental, something elusive, was wrong.

The New Deal had accomplished a heart-warming relief of distress, it had achieved a certain measure of recovery, it had released great forces of mass protest and had revived American liberalism,

it had left upon the statute books several measures of permanent value, it had established the principle that the entire community through the agency of the federal government has some responsibility for mass welfare, and it had impressed its values so deeply upon the national mind that the Republicans were compelled to endorse its major accomplishments in election platforms. But, as Roosevelt was aware, it had failed to realize his objectives of distributive justice and sound, stable prosperity.[9]

In April 1938 Roosevelt adopted two expedients that signalized the severity of the crisis in the New Deal: one was a return to spending on a large scale, the other a crusade against monopoly. The first expedient solved the immediate crisis: Congress readily appropriated new funds, business conditions responded quickly, and the "Roosevelt recession" was soon liquidated. Henceforth Roosevelt took it for granted that the economy could not operate without the stimulus of government funds. In his memorable budget message of 1940 he finally accepted in theory what he had long been doing in fact, admitted the responsibility of government retrenchment for the recession, credited the revival of spending for the revival in business, and in general discussed the problem of the federal budget in Keynesian terms.[10]

The second expedient, the call for an attack upon monopoly, was a complete reversal of Roosevelt's philosophy of 1933

[9] Cf. the comment of Professor Tugwell in *The Stricken Land:* "It was in economics that our troubles lay. For their solution his progressivism, his new deal, was pathetically insufficient. . . . I think . . . that he will be put down as having failed in this realm of [domestic] affairs."

[10] The Hoover administration, which Roosevelt had accused of extravagance in 1932, was now criticized for having failed to spend enough to fight the depression.

and the NRA policy. The message to Congress in which the crusade was announced — and which led to the fruitful TNEC investigations — was one of the most remarkable economic documents that have ever come from the White House. Roosevelt viewed the structure of economic and political power in broad social perspective. "Private power," he declared, was reaching a point at which it became "stronger than the democratic state itself." In the United States "a concentration of private power without equal in history is growing," which is "seriously impairing the effectiveness of private enterprise." "Private enterprise is ceasing to be free enterprise and is becoming a cluster of private collectivisms." A democratic people would no longer accept the meager standards of living caused by the failure of monopolistic industry to produce. "Big business collectivism in industry compels an ultimate collectivism in government." "The power of the few to manage the economic life of the Nation must be diffused among the many or be transferred to the public and its democratically responsible government."

Like Wilson, Roosevelt saw the development of big business and monopoly as a menace to democratic institutions, but like Wilson and all other politicians who touched upon the so-called trust problem, he was equivocal about how this menace was to be controlled. Although his argument carried to the brink of socialism, it was not socialism that he was proposing. Nor did he propose to reverse the whole modern trend of economic integration by trying to dissolve big business, a course of action the futility of which had been demonstrated by almost fifty years of experience. The econo-

mists whose guidance he was following believed that the rigid price structure of the semi-monopolized heavy industries was throwing the whole economy out of gear. Presumably anti-trust measures were not to be used to break up big corporations but to discipline their pricing policies. How the reformist state was to police the corporations without either destroying private enterprise or itself succumbing to the massed strength of corporate opposition was not made clear. Roosevelt did not tackle such problems in theory, and events spared him the necessity of facing them in practice.

Roosevelt's sudden and desperate appeal to the ancient trustbusting device, together with his failure in the fall elections of 1938 to purge the conservative elements in his party, augured the political bankruptcy of the New Deal. The reform wave had spent itself, and the Democratic Party, divided by the Supreme Court fight and the purge and hamstrung by its large conservative bloc, was exhausted as an agency of reform. Always the realist, Roosevelt rang the death knell of the New Deal in his annual message to Congress on January 4, 1939. "We have now passed the period of internal conflict in the launching of our program of social reform," he declared. "Our full energies may now be released to invigorate the processes of recovery in order to preserve our reforms." Almost three years before Pearl Harbor his experimentation had run its course. "The processes of recovery" came only with war. "Our full energies" were never successfully released for peacetime production. What would have happened to the political fortunes of Franklin D. Roosevelt if the war had not created a new theater for his leadership?

Suggestions for Additional Reading

Although we are only a few years away from the age of Roosevelt, a very considerable number of works dealing with the New Deal, or special aspects of it, have already appeared. Not many writers, however, have attempted as yet a comprehensive treatment of the New Deal era. Among the general works which have been written are Charles and Mary Beard, *America in Midpassage* (New York, 1939); Dixon Wecter, *The Age of the Great Depression, 1929–1941* (New York, 1948); and Broadus Mitchell, *Depression Decade* (New York, 1947).

A rapidly growing number of memoirs and autobiographical works written by many of the leading personalities associated with Roosevelt have appeared in the last ten or fifteen years. Frances Perkins's *The Roosevelt I Knew* (New York, 1946) is generally considered to be the best of these works because her sympathetic examination of Roosevelt is controlled by detachment and intelligent awareness of a context larger than the loves and hates of Washington officialdom. Other notable books in this category which are less favorable to Roosevelt are Raymond Moley, *After Seven Years* (New York, 1939); James A. Farley, *Jim Farley's Story* (New York, 1948); Cordell Hull, *The Memoirs of Cordell Hull* (New York, 1948, 2 vols.). Additional material on the character and personality of Franklin D. Roosevelt is furnished by some recent books of a biographical or quasi-biographical nature, such as Elliott Roosevelt, *As He Saw It* (New York, 1946); Robert Sherwood, *Roosevelt and Hopkins* (New York, 1948); John T. Flynn, *The Roosevelt Myth* (New York, 1948); and Gerald Johnson, *Roosevelt: Dictator or Democrat?* (New York, 1941).

Many useful works have also appeared dealing with special phases of the New Deal. Particular aspects of the economic and social program of the New Deal are studied in such works as E. G. Nourse, J. S. Davis, and J. D. Black, *Three Years of the Agricultural Adjustment Administration* (Washington, 1937); Joseph S. Davis, *On Agricultural Policy, 1926–1938* (Stanford University, 1939); Hugh S. Johnson, *The Blue Eagle, from Egg to Earth* (Garden City, New York, 1935); David E. Lilienthal, *T.V.A.: Democracy on the March* (New York, 1944); Paul H. Douglas, *Social Security in the United States* (New York, 1936); R. R. R. Brooks, *Unions of Their Own Choosing* (New Haven, 1939); Joseph Rosenfarb, *The National Labor Policy and How It Works* (New York, 1940); Donald S. Howard, *The W.P.A. and Federal Relief Policy* (New York, 1943).

The new relationship between public administration and the American economy is particularly well developed in Merle Fainsod and Lincoln Gordon, *Government and the American Economy* (New York, 1941). The constitutional issues of the New Deal are examined in Robert Jackson, *The Struggle for Judicial Supremacy* (New York, 1941); Edward S. Corwin, *The Twilight of the Supreme Court* (New Haven, 1934); R. K. Carr,

The Supreme Court and Judicial Review (New York, 1942).

No one can really get the "feel" of the New Deal era and a satisfactory insight into its impact on the minds of Americans without reading many of the newspaper editorials, magazine articles, and literary works of the period. A well-chosen collection of such writings is Milton Crane's *The Roosevelt Era* (New York, 1947).

For those who wish to let Franklin D. Roosevelt speak for himself, there is *The Public Papers and Addresses of Franklin D. Roosevelt*, ed. Samuel I. Rosenman (New York, 1938–1941, 9 vols.).

DATE DUE